— *the* —
COMMON
GOSPEL

— *the* —
COMMON
GOSPEL

the Ultimate Testament
to Jesus the Messiah

THE FOUR EVANGELISTS
MATTHEW, MARK, LUKE & JOHN

MILLENNIUM READER'S EDITION

Published by Wordsmith Associates
Geneva, Illinois

The Four Evangelists *(Matthew, Mark, Luke & John)*
The Common Gospel –
The Ultimate Testament to Jesus the Messiah
MILLENNIUM READER'S EDITION, Updated
R. M. MEBANE, Editor
Geneva, Illinois / Wordsmith Associates / 2006
330 pp / ISBN 978-0-9759290-4-9

BISAC Subject Codes:

BIB000000	*Bibles: General*
REL070000	*Religion: Christianity - General*
REL006160	*Religion: Biblical Reference - General*

22 21 19 18   10 9 8 7 6 5 4 3 2

Wordsmith Associates, Publisher
1400 Sherwood Lane
Geneva, Illinois 60134
United States of America

RMEBANE@WORDSMITH.ASSOCIATES
HTTPS://WORDSMITH.ASSOCIATES

*The Beginning of the Good News
of Jesus the Messiah, Son of God*

About This Book

The Common Gospel presents the Good News of Jesus the Messiah, Son of God, in a single, unified book.

This is significant because the Good News is traditionally expressed in four books, called the Gospels According to Matthew, Mark, Luke and John. They are typically bound together in the Christian Bible as the first four books of the New Testament. Simply stated, *The Common Gospel* connects these four sources and unifies the individual accounts within one common, organized framework.

Gospel Significance and Challenge

The four Gospels are foundational works that ground our knowledge of Jesus. When they were written almost two thousand years ago, the Gospels were instrumental in coalescing faith in Jesus as the Messiah and Son of God. In the centuries since, the Gospels have become canonized in the Christian church and are now accepted around the world as the authoritative sources of testimony regarding the times and teachings of Jesus. As such, the Gospels stand among the most influential works in the history of humankind.

Along with this importance, there is an enigmatic quality to the Gospels that stems from their divergence. While the Gospels share a sense of purpose and destiny, they developed along divergent paths. The Gospel scribes wrote in different times and places, they had different original sources available to them, and they applied distinct interpretive lenses. Consequently, they address different things, at varying levels of detail and emphasis. Even where there is commonality of subject matter, the account segments are scrambled, and facts and circumstances occasionally seem to conflict. The extraordinary legacy of the Gospel writers is one of four unreconciled perspectives presented in an unfinished language form.

While great insight and significance may be found in the differences among the Gospels, the divergence makes them difficult to read and understand. To many well-intentioned readers, the Gospels seem all tangled up, and it is a genuine struggle to unravel the threads. In a visual sense, reading the Gospels is like looking through four separate frames of stained glass, exquisitely sculpted by hand. The views through the panes form a wondrous montage that is rich with color and deep with meaning but that is also complex and challenging to behold.

The Common Gospel

Against this backdrop, *The Common Gospel* aims with fidelity and precision to bridge the divergent paths, to reconcile the different perspectives, and to recast the glass in a manner that presents a panoramic view in sharp and penetrating focus.

On one level, *The Common Gospel* simplifies and clarifies the presentation. In establishing a proper union of the four original texts, it takes nothing away, other than redundant words. Instead, it takes the original Gospels and organizes the language so that it flows naturally in manageable segments along a coherent, continuous story line. In the process, *The Common Gospel* adds organization and structure, softens shifts in emphasis and tone, and reconciles conflicting recollections. It presents the biblical history of Jesus in a form that is well organized, clear and complete.

On another level, *The Common Gospel* brings a sense of conclusion by extending original Gospel premises to create a full and final integration. The Gospel writers created their enduring records by skillfully piecing together segments from other manuscripts and stories passed by word of mouth within the early Christian communities. In so doing, the scribes sought to establish a testimonial basis for matters related to Jesus to be "known with certainty," so that people would come to believe in Jesus as the Son of God and thereby "have life in his name."

In similar fashion, *The Common Gospel* deliberately pieces together language segments to foster understanding and belief. However, by working exclusively with the four Gospels – themselves the accepted sources of biblical truth – *The Common Gospel* presents an inclusive synthesis of authentic original testimony and, in this convergence, effectively completes the evolution of the ancient texts.

What follows, then, are the Gospel offerings of Matthew, Mark, Luke and John, ultimately combined with meticulous editorial care to elucidate the Word. With the facets of the four gemstones thus aligned, the light of God may be seen to radiate in all directions – startling in its brilliance, stunning in its power.

R. M. MEBANE, Editor
December 2005

Since many have undertaken to set a narrative in order concerning those matters that have been fulfilled among us — just as those who were eyewitnesses and servants of the Word from the beginning delivered them to us — it seemed good also, having traced the course of all things accurately from the first, to compose an account so that these things are known with certainty. It is written so that you may believe that Jesus is the Son of God and that, believing, you may have life in his name.

— the —

COMMON GOSPEL

CONTENTS

MAP OF
THE REGION

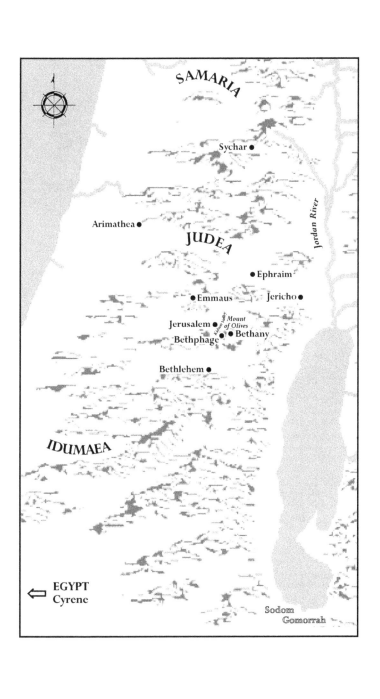

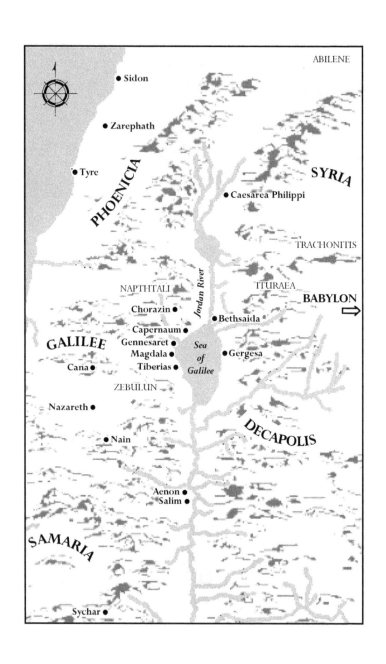

FOREWORD

Eternal Word

IN THE BEGINNING WAS the Word, and the Word was with God, and the Word was God.

He was in the beginning with God. All things were made through him, and nothing has been made without him. In him was life, and the life was the light of all people.

The light shines in the darkness, and the darkness has not overcome it.

❧

The Word became flesh and lived among us. We saw his glory, such glory as of the one and only Son of the Father, full of grace and truth. From his fullness we have all received grace upon grace.

The law was given through Moses, but grace and truth came through Jesus the Messiah. No one has seen God at any time. The one and only Son, who is in the bosom of the Father, has declared him.

❧

He was in the world, and the world was made through him, yet the world did not recognize him. He came to his own, and those who were his own did not receive him.

But to as many as received him, to those who believed in his name, he gave the right to become God's children, born not of blood, nor of the will of the flesh, nor of the will of man, but of God.

Part 1

BIRTH AND
FIRST YEARS

BIRTH AND FIRST YEARS

An account of events related to
the birth and first years of Jesus the Messiah

Part 1

An angel appears to Zacharias

IN THE DAYS OF Herod, the king of Judea, there was a certain priest named Zacharias, of the priestly division of Abijah. He had a wife of the daughters of Aaron, and her name was Elizabeth. They were both righteous before God, walking blamelessly in all the commandments and ordinances of the Lord. They lived in a Judean city in the hill country. But they had no child, because Elizabeth was barren, and they both were well advanced in years.

※❀⁂

Now it happened, while Zacharias executed the priest's office before God in the order of his division according to the custom, his lot was to enter into the temple of the Lord and burn incense. As he did, an angel of the Lord appeared to him, standing on the right side of the altar of incense.

Zacharias was troubled when he saw him, and fear fell upon him. But the angel said,

Do not be afraid, Zacharias, because your request has been heard. Your wife, Elizabeth, will bear you a son, and you shall call him *John*. You will have joy and gladness. Even from his mother's womb, he will be filled with the Holy Spirit, and many will rejoice at his birth, for he will be great in the sight of the Lord.

In the spirit and power of Elijah, he will go before God to turn the hearts of parents to their children and the disobedient to the wisdom of the just, to make ready a people prepared for the Lord. He will turn many of the children of Israel to the Lord their God.

Zacharias doubted the angel. He said, "How can I be sure of this? I am an old man, and my wife is well advanced in years."

The angel answered him, "I am Gabriel, who stands in the presence of God. I was sent to speak to you and to bring you this good news. Behold, because you did not believe my words, which will be fulfilled in their proper time, you will not be able to speak. You will be silent until the day that these things happen."

The whole multitude of the people praying outside were waiting for Zacharias, and they marveled that he delayed in the temple.

When he came out, he could not speak to them. He continued making signs to them and remained mute.

They perceived that he had seen a vision in the temple.

꙰

When the days of Zacharias' service were fulfilled, he departed to his house and, after these days, his wife, Elizabeth, conceived.

She said, "Thus has the Lord done to me in the days in which he looked at me, to take away my reproach among men."

Elizabeth hid herself for five months.

An angel appears to Mary

One month after Elizabeth came out of seclusion, the angel Gabriel was sent from God to Nazareth, a city of Galilee, to a virgin named Mary.

Having come in, the angel said to her, "Rejoice, you highly favored one. The Lord is with you. Blessed are you among women."

Greatly troubled at these words, Mary considered what kind of salutation this might be. And the angel said to her,

Do not be afraid, Mary, for you have found favor with God. Behold, you will conceive in your womb and bring forth a son, and you will name him *Jesus*.

He will be great and will be called the Son of the Most High, and the Lord God will give him the throne of his father, David. He will reign over the house of Jacob forever. There will be no end to his kingdom.

Mary asked the angel, "How can this be, seeing that I am a virgin?"

The angel answered her, "Everything spoken by God is possible. Behold Elizabeth, your relative, in her old age and called barren, also has conceived a son. The Holy Spirit will come on you, and the power of the Most High will overshadow you. Therefore, the holy one who is born from you will also be called the Son of God."

Mary said, "Behold, I am the handmaid of the Lord. Let it be done to me according to your word."

Then the angel departed from her.

An angel appears to Joseph

When Mary was found to be pregnant by the Holy Spirit, she was pledged to be married to a man whose name was Joseph, of the house of David, but it was before they came together.

Joseph, being a righteous man and not willing to make her a public example, intended to put her away secretly. But while he thought about these things, behold, an angel of the Lord appeared to him in a dream, saying,

> **Do not be afraid, Joseph, son of David, to take Mary to yourself as your wife, for that which is conceived in her is of the Holy Spirit.**

> **She shall bring forth a son, and you shall call his name *Jesus,* for it is he who shall save his people from their sins.**

Joseph arose from his sleep and did as the angel of the Lord commanded him. He took Mary as his wife, but did not know her sexually until she had brought forth her firstborn son.

Mary visits Elizabeth

In those days, Mary went with haste into the hill country of Judea, to the house of Zacharias, where she stayed for about three months before returning to her home.

She entered into the house and greeted Elizabeth. Elizabeth was filled with the Holy Spirit and called out with a loud voice, "Blessed are you among women, and blessed is the fruit of your womb. For behold, when the voice of your greeting came into my ears, the baby leaped in my womb for joy. Why am I so favored, that the mother of my Lord should come to me? Blessed is she who believed, for there will be a fulfillment of the things which have been spoken to her from the Lord."

Mary said,

> **My soul magnifies the Lord. My spirit has rejoiced in God my savior, for he has looked at the humble state of his handmaid. Behold, from now on, all generations will call me blessed, for he who is mighty has done great things for me. Holy is his name.**

His mercy is for generations of generations on those who fear him. He has shown strength with his arm. He has scattered the proud in the imagination of their hearts. He has put down princes from their thrones and has exalted the lowly. He has filled the hungry with good things, and he has sent the rich away empty.

He has given help to his servant, Israel, so that mercy might be remembered as he spoke to our fathers, to Abraham, and to his seed forever.

John is born

Now the time that Elizabeth should give birth was fulfilled, and she brought forth a son. Her neighbors and her relatives heard that the Lord had magnified his mercy toward her, and they rejoiced with her.

On the eighth day, they came to circumcise the child, and they would have called him Zacharias, after the name of the father. But his mother said, "Not so, he will be called *John.*"

They said to her, "There is no one among your relatives who is called by this name." They made signs to his father to discover what he would have him called. They all marveled – Zacharias asked for a writing tablet, and wrote, "His name is *John.*"

Immediately, his mouth opened, his tongue was freed, and he spoke, blessing God.

Fear came on all who lived around them, and all these words were talked about throughout the hill country of Judea. The hand of the Lord was with this child, and all who heard these things laid them up in their heart, saying, "What then will this child be?"

His father, Zacharias, filled with the Holy Spirit, prophesied, saying,

Blessed be the Lord, the God of Israel, for he has visited and worked redemption for his people. He has raised up a horn of salvation for us in the house of his servant David – salvation from our enemies and from the hand of all who hate us.

So doing, he has shown mercy toward our forebears, reminding us of his holy covenant – the oath which he spoke to our father, Abraham – to grant that, being delivered out of the hand of our enemies, we should serve him without fear, in holiness and righteousness before him all the days of our life.

And you, child, will be called a prophet of the Most High, for you will go before the face of the Lord to make ready his ways, to give knowledge of salvation to his people by the remission of their sins.

From the tender mercy of our God, the dawn from on high will visit us – to shine on those who sit in darkness and the shadow of death, to guide our feet into the way of peace.

⁕ᘛ⃰ᘚ⁕

The child grew. He never drank wine or strong drink, and he became strong in spirit. He was in the desert until the day of his public appearance to Israel.

Jesus the Messiah is born

Now the birth of Jesus the Messiah happened in this way.

A decree went out from Caesar Augustus that all the world should be enrolled. This was the first enrollment made when Quirinius was governor of Syria. All were to go to their own cities to enroll themselves.

Because Joseph was of the house and family of David, he went out from Galilee, from the city of Nazareth, into Judea, to the city of David, which is called Bethlehem. Joseph went to enroll himself with Mary, who was pregnant.

While they were there, the day came for her to give birth, and she brought forth her firstborn son.

She wrapped him in bands of cloth and, because there was no room for them in the inn, she laid him in a manger.

Shepherds seek the Child

In the same country, there were shepherds staying in the field, keeping watch by night over their flock, when an angel of the Lord came to stand by them and the glory of the Lord shone around them.

They were terrified, but the angel said to them,

Do not be afraid, for, behold, I bring you good news of great joy, which will be to all the people. There is born to you, this day, in the city of David, a savior, who is the Messiah, the Lord.

This is the sign to you – you will find a baby wrapped in strips of cloth, lying in a manger.

Suddenly, a multitude of the heavenly host was there with the angel, praising God and saying,

Glory to God in the highest and, on earth, peace and good will toward all people.

When the angels went away from them into the sky, the shepherds said one to another, "Let us go to Bethlehem now and see this thing that has happened, which the Lord has made known to us."

They came with haste and found both Mary and Joseph, and the baby was lying in the manger.

When they saw it, they widely publicized the words spoken to them about this child. All who heard it wondered at these things, but Mary kept all these sayings, pondering them in her heart.

The shepherds returned, glorifying and praising God for all the things that they had heard and seen, just as it was told them.

The Holy Family visits Jerusalem

When eight days were fulfilled for the circumcision of the child, he was called *Jesus,* as was given by the angel before he was conceived in the womb.

When the days of their purification according to the law of Moses were fulfilled, Joseph and Mary brought him up to Jerusalem, to present him to the Lord, as it is written in the law of the Lord, "Every male who opens the womb shall be called holy to the Lord." They offered a sacrifice of two turtledoves according to that law.

⁕⁂⁕

Behold, there was a man in Jerusalem whose name was Simeon. The Holy Spirit was on him, and he was righteous and devout, looking for the consolation of Israel. It had been revealed to him by the Holy Spirit that he should not see death before he had seen the Lord's Messiah.

He came in the Spirit into the temple. When the parents brought in the child, Jesus, Simeon received him into his arms and blessed God and said,

Master, you are now releasing your servant, according to your word, in peace. My eyes have seen your salvation, which you have prepared before the face of all peoples – a light for revelation to the nations and the glory of your people Israel.

Joseph and his mother were marveling at the things which were spoken concerning him.

Simeon blessed them and said to the mother, Mary,

Behold, this child is set for the falling and the rising of many in Israel and for a sign which is spoken against. Yes, the thoughts of many hearts may be revealed, and a sword will pierce through your own soul.

※※※

There was also a prophetess, Anna, the daughter of Phanuel, of the tribe of Asher. She was of a great age, having lived with a husband seven years from her virginity, and she had been a widow for about eighty-four years. She did not depart from the temple, worshipping with fastings and petitions night and day.

At that very hour, she gave thanks to the Lord and spoke of him to all those who were looking for redemption in Jerusalem.

Magi seek the Child

Some time after Jesus was born in Bethlehem of Judea, behold, magi from the east came to Jerusalem, saying, "Where is he who is born King of the Jews? We saw his star in the east and have come to worship him."

※※※

When Herod the king heard it, he was troubled, and all Jerusalem was troubled with him.

Gathering together all the chief priests and scribes of the people, he asked them where the Messiah would be born.

They said to him, "In Bethlehem of Judea, for thus it is written through the prophet, 'You Bethlehem, land of Judah, are in no way least among the princes of Judah – for out of you shall come forth a governor, who shall shepherd my people, Israel.'"

Herod secretly called the magi and learned from them exactly what time the star appeared. Then he sent them to Bethlehem, and said, "Go and search diligently for the young child. When you have found him, bring me word, so that I also may come and worship him."

⁂

Having heard the king, the magi went their way and, behold, the star which they saw in the east stood over where the young child was.

When they saw the star, they rejoiced with exceedingly great joy. They came into the house and saw the young child with Mary, his mother, and they fell down and worshiped him. From among their treasures, they offered him gifts of gold, frankincense, and myrrh.

⁂

Warned in a dream that they should not return to Herod, they went back to their own country another way.

When Herod saw that he was mocked by the magi, he was exceedingly angry and sent out an order to kill all the male children who were in Bethlehem and in all the surrounding countryside, from two years old and under, according to the exact time which he had learned from the magi.

The Holy Family departs for Egypt

After the magi had departed, behold, an angel of the Lord appeared to Joseph in a dream, saying,

Arise and take the young child and his mother, and flee into Egypt, and stay there until I tell you, for Herod will seek the young child to destroy him.

He arose and took the young child and his mother by night, and departed into Egypt and was there until the death of Herod.

The Child grows

When Herod was dead, behold, an angel of the Lord appeared in a dream to Joseph in Egypt, saying,

Arise and take the young child and his mother, and go into the land of Israel, for those who sought the young child's life are dead.

He arose and took the young child and his mother, and came into the land of Israel. But, when he heard that Archelaus was reigning over Judea in the place of his father, Herod, he was afraid to go there. So they returned to the region of Galilee, to their own city, Nazareth. The child grew, became strong in spirit, filled with wisdom, and the grace of God was upon him.

Young Jesus learns

Every year his parents went to Jerusalem at the feast of the Passover with the boy Jesus and, when he was twelve years old, they went up to Jerusalem according to the custom of the feast.

When they had fulfilled the days, as they were returning, Jesus stayed behind in Jerusalem, but Joseph and his mother did not know it.

Supposing him to be in the company, they went a day's journey. They looked for him among their relatives and acquaintances and, when they did not find him, they returned to Jerusalem, looking for him.

After three days they found him in the temple, sitting in the midst of the teachers, both listening to them and asking them questions. All who heard him were amazed at his understanding.

When they saw him, they were astonished, and his mother said to him, "Son, why have you treated us this way? Behold, your father and I were anxiously looking for you."

He said to them, "Why were you looking for me? Did you not know that I must be in my Father's house?" They did not understand what he said to them.

⁕ﷺ⁕

He went with them to Nazareth and was subject to them. His mother kept all these sayings in her heart.

And Jesus increased in wisdom and stature, in human favor and in favor with God.

Part 2

SANCTIFICATION

SANCTIFICATION

An account of events related to
the sanctification of Jesus the Messiah

Part 2

John prepares the way

THERE CAME A MAN sent from God whose name was John. He came as a witness, so that he might testify about the light, that all might believe through him. He was not the light, but was sent to testify about the light. The true light that enlightens everyone was coming into the world.

John is the one who was spoken of by Isaiah the prophet, as he said,

> **Behold, I send my messenger before you, to prepare your way –** **the voice of one crying in the wilderness,** *Make ready the way of the* *Lord. Make his paths straight. Every valley will be filled. Every mountain* *and hill will be brought low. The crooked will become straight and the* *rough ways made smooth. All flesh will see the salvation of God.*

᠅⚜᠅

When the word of God came to John, son of Zacharias, in the wilderness of Judea, it was in the fifteenth year of the reign of Tiberius Caesar. It was when Pontius Pilate was governor of Judea, Herod was tetrarch of Galilee, Herod's brother Philip was tetrarch of the region of Ituraea and Trachonitis, and Lysanias was tetrarch of Abilene. It was in the high priesthood of Annas and Caiaphas.

John baptizes in the wilderness

In those days, John baptized in the wilderness of Judea, saying, "Repent, for the kingdom of heaven is at hand." He wore clothing made of camel's hair, with a leather belt around his waist. He ate locusts and wild honey.

He traveled in all the region around the Jordan, proclaiming the baptism of repentance for forgiveness of sins.

People from Jerusalem and all of Judea went out to him and, confessing their sins, were baptized by him in the Jordan River.

❀⚜❀

Once, when he saw many of the Pharisees and Sadducees coming for his baptism, he said to them,

> You offspring of vipers, who warned you to flee from the wrath to come? Bring forth fruit worthy of repentance. Do not begin to say among yourselves, *We have Abraham for our father,* for I tell you, God is able to raise up children to Abraham from these stones.
>
> Even now the axe lies at the root of the trees. Every tree, therefore, that does not bring forth good fruit is cut down and thrown into the fire.

The crowds asked him, "What then must we do?" And he answered, "Whoever has two coats should give one to any who has none. Whoever has spare food should do likewise."

Tax collectors also came to be baptized, and they said to him, "Teacher, what must we do?" He said to them, "Collect no more than that which is appointed to you."

Even soldiers asked him, "What about us? What must we do?" And he said to them, "Extort from no one by violence, neither accuse anyone wrongfully, and be content with your wages."

❀⚜❀

As the people were expectant, they wondered in their hearts about John, whether perhaps he was the Messiah.

This is the testimony of John when the Jews sent priests and Levites from Jerusalem to ask him, "Who are you?"

He confessed who he was and did not deny, but he confessed, "I am not the Messiah."

They asked him, "What then? Are you Elijah?" And he said, "I am not."

They asked, "Are you the prophet?" And he answered, "No."

Then they said to him, "Who are you? Give us an answer to take back to those who sent us. What do you say about yourself?"

He said in a manner of Isaiah the prophet,

> I am the voice of one crying in the wilderness, *Make straight the way of the Lord.*

Having been sent from the Pharisees, they asked him, "Why then do you baptize if you are not the Messiah, nor Elijah, nor the prophet?"

John answered them all,

> Among you stands one whom you do not know. He is the one who comes after me and is mightier than I. I am not worthy to carry his shoes or even to stoop down and loosen the thong of his sandals.

> I baptize in water for repentance, but he will baptize you in the Holy Spirit and with fire. His winnowing fork is in his hand, and he will thoroughly cleanse his threshing floor and gather the wheat into his barn. But he will burn up the chaff with unquenchable fire.

Then, with many other exhortations, he proclaimed good news to the people.

John baptizes Jesus

One day Jesus came from Nazareth of Galilee to John at the Jordan.

John himself did not know him, but the one who sent him to baptize in water said to him, "On whomever you see the Spirit descend and remain, it is he who baptizes in the Holy Spirit." And John came baptizing in water for this reason – that this one would be revealed to Israel.

As Jesus came toward him, John saw the Spirit descending like a dove out of heaven, and it remained on him – and John saw that this was the Son of God. He testified,

Behold the Lamb of God, who takes away the sin of the world. This is he of whom I said, *After me comes a man who has surpassed me and is preferred before me, for he was before me.*

༈

Jesus came from Galilee to be baptized by John, and John would have hindered him, saying, "I need to be baptized by you, and yet you come to me?" But Jesus answered him,

Allow it now, for this is the fitting way for us to fulfill all righteousness.

Then John so allowed, and Jesus was baptized.

༈

After Jesus was baptized by John in the Jordan, immediately as he came up from the water, he saw the heavens parting, and the Spirit of God again descended on him like a dove.

And a voice out of the heavens said,

You are my beloved Son. In you I am well pleased.

Jesus is tempted by the devil

Jesus, full of the Holy Spirit, returned from the Jordan, and immediately the Spirit drove him out into the wilderness, with the wild animals, to be tempted by the devil.

He fasted forty days and forty nights – he ate nothing – and afterward, when those days were completed, he was hungry.

ꙮ

The tempter came and said to him,

If you are the Son of God, command that these stones become bread.

Jesus answered him,

It is written, *A person shall not live by bread alone, but by every word that proceeds from the mouth of God.*

ꙮ

Then the devil took him to the holy city of Jerusalem, set him on the pinnacle of the temple, and said to him,

If you are the Son of God, throw yourself down from here, for it is written, *He will put his angels in charge of you, to guard you,* and, *On their hands they will bear you up, so that you do not dash your foot against a stone.*

Jesus answered him,

Again, it is written, *You shall not test the Lord, your God.*

❦

The devil then took him up on an exceedingly high mountain and showed him all the kingdoms of the world and their glory in a moment of time.

The devil said to him,

I will give you their glory and all this authority, for it has been delivered to me, and I give it to whomever I want. I will give you all of these things, it will all be yours if you will fall down and worship me.

Jesus said to him,

Get behind me, Satan, for it is written, *You shall worship the Lord your God, and you shall serve him only.*

❦

The devil had completed every temptation and left him then, departing until another time.

And, behold, angels came and served Jesus.

Jesus spreads the good news

From there, Jesus, in the power of the Spirit, went about throughout Galilee, teaching in synagogues, proclaiming the good news of the kingdom, and healing every disease and sickness among the people. News about him spread through all the surrounding area, and he was glorified by all.

Part 3

EARLY PASSAGE

EARLY PASSAGE

An account of events related to
the early passage of Jesus the Messiah

Part 3

Jesus gives first sign in Cana

JESUS WAS ABOUT THIRTY years old when he began to teach.

⁓❦⁓

One day, there was a marriage in Cana of Galilee, and Jesus was invited. He came with his disciples, and the mother of Jesus was also there.

When the wine ran out, Jesus' mother said to him, "They have no wine."

Jesus said to her, "Woman, what does that have to do with you and me? My hour has not yet come."

His mother said to the servants, "Do whatever he says to you."

Now there were six stone water pots, set there after the Jews' manner of purifying, each containing two or three metretes apiece. Jesus said to them, "Fill the water pots with water." And they filled them up to the brim. Then he said to them, "Now draw some out, and take it to the ruler of the feast." So they took it.

The water now became wine, and the ruler of the feast tasted it. Though the servants who had drawn the water knew where it came from, the ruler of the feast did not, and he called the bridegroom and said, "Everyone serves the good wine first and then, when the guests have drunk freely, that which is worse. But you have kept the good wine until now."

⁓❦⁓

Jesus did this – the beginning of his signs – in Cana of Galilee and revealed his glory, and his disciples believed in him.

After this, he went down to Capernaum, with his mother, his brothers, and his disciples, and they stayed there for some time.

Jesus gives signs in Jerusalem

When Passover of the Jews was at hand, Jesus traveled to Jerusalem. During the Passover feast, many observed signs that he did and believed in his name.

But Jesus did not entrust himself to them, because he knew everyone – what was in them – and he did not need for anyone to testify concerning anyone else.

※✳✳✳※

In the temple he found those who sold oxen, sheep, and doves, and the changers of money sitting down.

He made a whip of cords, and threw all the sheep and oxen out of the temple, and he poured out the changers' money and overthrew their tables.

To those who sold the doves, he said, "Take these things out of here. Do not make my Father's house a marketplace."

The Jews then asked him, "What sign do you show us, seeing that you do these things?"

Jesus answered them, "Destroy this temple, and in three days I will raise it up."

The Jews said, "This temple was in building for forty-six years, and you will raise it up in three days?"

But he was speaking of the temple of his body.

Jesus answers Nicodemus

Now there was a Pharisee named Nicodemus, a ruler of the Jews. He came to Jesus by night and said to him, "Rabbi, we know that you are a teacher from God, for no one can do these signs that you do unless God is with him."

Jesus said to him,

Truly I tell you, one cannot see the kingdom of God unless born anew.

Nicodemus asked him, "How can anyone be born after growing old? Can one enter a second time into the mother's womb and be born?"

Jesus answered,

Truly I tell you, one cannot enter into the kingdom of God unless born of water and spirit. That which is born of the flesh is flesh. That which is born of the Spirit is spirit.

Do not marvel that I say to you, *You must be born anew.* The wind blows where it wants to, and you hear its sound but do not know where it comes from and where it is going. So it is for everyone who is born of the Spirit.

Nicodemus answered him, "How can these things be?" And Jesus answered him,

You are the teacher of Israel and do not understand these things?

Truly I tell you, we speak of that which we know and testify to that which we have seen, and you do not receive our witness. If I tell you earthly things and you do not believe, how will you believe if I tell you heavenly things?

No one ascends into heaven but he who descends out of heaven – the Son of Man. As Moses lifted up the serpent in the wilderness, even so must the Son of Man be lifted up, that whoever believes in him should not perish, but have eternal life.

꧁꧂

After these things, Jesus went with his disciples into the land of Judea. He stayed there with them and baptized.

John baptizes at Aenon

John was baptizing at Aenon near Salim because there was much water there. People came and were baptized.

There arose a questioning on the part of John's disciples with some Jews about purification. They came to John and said to him, "Rabbi, he who was with you beyond the Jordan – to whom you have testified – behold, he baptizes, and everyone is coming to him."

John answered,

No one can receive anything unless it has been given from heaven. You yourselves testify that I said, *I am not the Messiah, but I have been sent before him.*

He who has the bride is the bridegroom. And the friend of the bridegroom, who stands and hears him, rejoices greatly at the bridegroom's voice. Therefore, my joy is made full. He must increase, but I must decrease.

The one who is from the earth belongs to the earth and speaks of the earth. The one who comes from heaven above is above all. He whom God has sent speaks the word of God, for God gives the Spirit without measure.

The Father loves the Son and has given all things into his hand. He testifies to what he has seen and heard, and whoever has received his witness has set the seal to this, that God is true, and whoever believes in the Son has eternal life. Whoever disobeys the Son will not see life, and on that one the wrath of God will remain.

Jesus meets a Samarian woman

When Jesus found out that the Pharisees had heard that he was making and baptizing more disciples than John, he left Judea and departed for Galilee. But he needed to pass through Samaria.

He came to a city of Samaria, called Sychar, near the parcel of ground that Jacob had given to his son, Joseph. Jacob's well was there and Jesus, being tired from his journey, sat down by the well. It was about the sixth hour, and his disciples had gone away into the city to buy food.

A woman of Samaria came to draw water, and Jesus said to her, "Give me a drink."

Since Jews have no dealings with Samaritans, the woman said to him, "How is it that you, being a Jew, ask for a drink from me, a woman of Samaria?"

Jesus answered her, "If you knew the gift of God and he who says to you, 'Give me a drink,' you would have asked him, and he would have given you living water."

The woman said to him, "Sir, you have nothing to draw with, and the well is deep. From where then would you have that living water? Are you greater than our ancestor, Jacob, who gave us the well and drank of it himself, as did his children and his livestock?"

Jesus answered her, "Everyone who drinks of this water will thirst again, but all who drink of the water that I will give them will never thirst again. The water that I give will become in them a well of water springing up to eternal life."

The woman said to him, "Sir, give me this water, so that I do not get thirsty and do not have to come all the way here to draw."

Jesus said to her, "Go, call your husband, and come here."

The woman answered, "I have no husband."

Jesus said to her, "You said well, 'I have no husband,' for you have had five husbands, and he whom you now have is not your husband. This you have said truly."

The woman said to him, "Sir, I perceive that you are a prophet. Our ancestors worshiped on this mountain, but you say that in Jerusalem is the place where people ought to worship."

Jesus said to her,

Woman, believe me, the hour comes when neither in this mountain nor in Jerusalem will you worship the Father.

You worship that which you do not know. We worship that which we know, for salvation is from the Jews. But the hour comes, and now is, when the true worshippers will worship the Father in spirit and truth, for the Father seeks such to be his worshippers.

God is Spirit, and those who worship him must worship in spirit and truth.

The woman said to him, "I know that the Messiah comes and, when he has come, he will declare to us all things."

Jesus said to her, "I am he, the one who speaks to you."

✺

At this time, his disciples came. They marveled that he was speaking with this woman, yet no one said, "What are you looking for?" or, "Why do you speak with her?"

✺

So the woman left her water pot and went away into the city. She said to the people, "Come, see a man who told me everything that I did. Can this be the Messiah?"

They went out of the city and were coming to him.

✺

Meanwhile, the disciples urged him, saying, "Rabbi, eat." But he said to them, "I have food to eat that you do not know about."

The disciples said one to another, "Has anyone brought him something to eat?"

Jesus said to them,

My food is to do the will of him who sent me and to accomplish his work.

Do you not say, *There are yet four months until the harvest?* Behold, I tell you, lift up your eyes and look at the fields – they are ripe for harvest already. The one who reaps receives wages and gathers

fruit for eternal life – both the one who sows and the one who reaps may rejoice together.

In this the saying is true, *One sows, and another reaps.* I sent you to reap that for which you have not labored. Others have labored, and you have entered into their labor.

✳✳✳

From that city, many of the Samaritans believed in him because of the word of the woman who testified, "He told me everything that I did." So when the Samaritans came to him, they begged him to stay with them, and he stayed there two days.

Many more believed because of his word. They said to the woman, "Now we believe, but not because of you. We have heard for ourselves and now know that this is indeed the savior of the world."

Jesus returns to Galilee

At the end of the two days, Jesus heard that John was delivered over, and he withdrew from there and went into Galilee.

When he came to Galilee, the Galileans received him, for they also went to the feast and saw all the things that he did in Jerusalem.

Then Jesus came again to Cana of Galilee, where he made the water into wine.

✳✳✳

There was a certain nobleman whose son was sick at Capernaum. When he heard that Jesus had come out of Judea into Galilee, he went to him and begged him to come and heal his son, for he was at the point of death.

Jesus said to him, "Unless you see signs and wonders, you will in no way believe."

The nobleman said to him, "Sir, come down before my child dies."

Jesus said to him, "Go your way. Your son lives."

The man believed the word that Jesus spoke to him, and he went his way. As he was going, his servants met him and reported, saying, "Your child lives."

He inquired of them the hour when he began to get better, and they said to him, "The fever left him yesterday at the seventh hour."

The father knew that it was at that hour in which Jesus said to him, "Your son lives."

He believed, as did his whole house.

❦

Jesus did this second sign in Cana after having come out of Judea back into Galilee.

Jesus enrages the Nazareans

After a time, Jesus came to Nazareth, where he had been brought up. As was his custom, he entered into the synagogue on the sabbath day.

He stood up to read, and the book of the prophet Isaiah was handed to him. He opened the book and found the place where it was written,

The Spirit of the Lord is on me, because he has anointed me to proclaim good news to the poor. He has sent me to proclaim release to the captives and the recovering of sight to the blind, to deliver those who are crushed, and to proclaim the acceptable year of the Lord.

He closed the book, gave it back to the attendant, and sat down. The eyes of all in the synagogue were fastened on him.

He began to tell them,

Today, this scripture has been fulfilled in your hearing.

All testified on his behalf and wondered at the gracious words which proceeded out of his mouth, and they said, "Is this not Joseph's son?"

He said to them,

Doubtless you will tell me this parable, *Physician, heal yourself,* and say, *Whatever we have heard done at Capernaum, do also here in your hometown.*

Then he said,

Truly I tell you, no prophet is acceptable in his hometown.

But truly I tell you, there were many widows in Israel in the days of Elijah, when the sky was shut up three years and six months and a great famine came over all the land. Elijah was sent to none of them except to a widow at Zarephath, in the land of Sidon.

There were many lepers in Israel in the time of Elisha the prophet, yet not one of them was cleansed except Naaman, the Syrian.

As they heard these things, all in the synagogue were filled with wrath.

They rose up, drove him out of the city, and led him to the brow of the hill on which their city was built, so that they might throw him off the cliff. But he went his way, passing through the midst of them.

᠃᠁ᢱᢕᢖᢕᢖᢱ᠁᠃

Testifying that a prophet has no honor in his own country, Jesus left Nazareth, and he came and lived in Capernaum by the sea, in the region of Zebulun and Naphtali.

From that time, Jesus began to proclaim the good news of the kingdom of God, saying, "The time is fulfilled, and the kingdom of heaven is at hand. Repent and believe in the good news."

Part 4

EXPRESSIONS OF POWER

EXPRESSIONS OF POWER

An account of events related to
expressions of power by Jesus the Messiah

Part 4

Jesus gathers adherents

WHILE JESUS WAS PASSING along by the sea of Galilee, near Gennesaret, and the crowd pressed on him to hear the word of God, he saw two fishermen – Andrew and his brother Simon – standing by their boats, washing their nets.

Andrew said to his brother, "We have found the Messiah," and he brought Simon to Jesus.

Jesus looked at him and said, "You are Simon, the son of Jonah. You shall be called Cephas."

※ᬉᬉ※

Then Jesus entered into one of the boats, that which was Simon's, and asked him to put out a short distance from the land.

He sat down and taught the crowds from the boat.

※ᬉᬉ※

When he had finished speaking, he said to Simon, "Put out into the deep and let down your nets for a catch."

Simon answered him, "Master, we worked all night and took nothing but, at your word, I will let down the nets."

When they did this, they caught a great multitude of fish, and their nets were breaking. They beckoned to their partners in another boat, that they should come and help them. The partners – James and John, sons of Zebedee – came, and they filled both boats until they began to sink.

Simon and all who were with him were amazed at the fish that they had caught. And Simon fell down at Jesus' knees, saying, "Depart from me, Lord, for I am a sinful man."

When they brought their boats to land, Jesus said to Simon, "Do not be afraid." To all, he said, "Come after me, and I will make you into fishers for people."

Immediately, Simon and his brother Andrew left their nets and followed him. James and his brother John left their boat with their father Zebedee and some hired servants and also followed Jesus.

※✬✬✬※

The next day, Jesus found Philip, who was from Bethsaida – the city of Andrew and Simon – and said to him, "Follow me."

Later, Philip found Nathanael and said to him, "We have found Jesus, the son of Joseph of Nazareth – the one of whom Moses and the prophets wrote in the law."

Nathanael said to him, "Can any good thing come out of Nazareth?"

Philip replied, "Come and see."

※✬✬✬※

Jesus saw Nathanael coming to him and said of him, "Behold, an Israelite indeed, in whom there is no deceit."

Nathanael said to him, "How do you know me?"

Jesus answered, "Before Philip called you, I saw you when you were under the fig tree."

Nathanael answered him, "Rabbi, you are the Son of God. You are King of Israel."

Jesus answered him, "Do you believe because I told you, 'I saw you underneath the fig tree'? If so, you will see greater things than these." Then he said to him,

Truly I tell you, hereafter you will see heaven opened and the angels of God ascending and descending on the Son of Man.

Jesus expels demons

On the sabbath day, he entered the synagogue and taught.

In the synagogue there was a man with the spirit of an unclean demon, and he cried out with a loud voice, "What have we to do with you, Jesus of Nazareth? Have you come to destroy us? I know who you are – the Holy One of God."

Jesus rebuked him, saying, "Be silent, and come out of him."

The demon threw him down in their midst and convulsed him, then came out of him, having done no harm.

They were all amazed, and they discussed this with one another, saying, "What are these words? A new teaching? With authority and power he commands even the unclean spirits, and they obey him – out they come."

Immediately, a report about him went out everywhere in the surrounding region of Galilee.

When they came out of the synagogue, they entered the house of Simon and Andrew, with James and John.

Now Simon's mother-in-law was afflicted with a great fever, and they told Jesus about her and they begged him to help her.

He came and stood over her and took her by the hand and raised her up. Then he rebuked the fever, and it left her. Immediately, she rose up and served them.

❦

That evening, when the sun was setting, all those who had any who were sick or possessed by demons brought them to him. The entire city was gathered together at the door.

Jesus laid his hands on every one of them and healed all who were sick and cast out the spirits with a word.

As the demons came out, many cried out, saying, "You are the Son of God." But he rebuked them and did not allow the demons to speak because they knew him – they knew that he was the Messiah.

Jesus extends healing powers

Early in the morning, while it was still dark, he rose up and departed to a deserted place and prayed there.

Simon and those with him followed and, when they found him, Simon said, "Everyone is looking for you."

When the crowds came to him, they held on to him, so that he would not go away.

But he said to them,

I must proclaim the good news of the kingdom of God. Let us go elsewhere into the next towns, so that I may proclaim there also, because I have been sent for this reason.

He went throughout all Galilee, proclaiming in the synagogues and casting out demons.

⁂

While Jesus was in one of the cities, behold, a man full of leprosy came to him. When he saw Jesus, he fell on his face in worship and begged him, "Lord, if you want to, you can make me clean."

Being moved with compassion, Jesus stretched out his hand and touched him, saying, "I want to. Be made clean." Immediately, the leprosy left him, and he was made clean.

Jesus sent him out and said to him, "See that you say nothing to anybody, but go show yourself to the priest and offer for your cleansing the gift that Moses commanded, as a testimony."

Instead he went out to proclaim it, and the report concerning him spread broadly.

Jesus could no longer openly enter a city. He stayed outside in desert places, and great crowds came to him from everywhere to be healed of their infirmities.

But he withdrew himself into the desert and prayed.

⁂

When Jesus came back to Capernaum after some days, people heard that he was in the house, and immediately many gathered together, so that there was no more room, not even around the door.

Jesus was teaching, speaking the word to them, and the power of the Lord was with him to heal. Pharisees and teachers of the law, who had come out of every village of Galilee and Judea, were there sitting by.

Four people came to him carrying a paralytic man, lying on a cot. They sought to bring him in to lie before Jesus. When they could not come near to him because of the crowd, they went up to the housetop and let him down on his cot through the tiles into the midst before Jesus.

Seeing their faith, Jesus said to the paralytic, "Son, take heart. Your sins are forgiven you."

The scribes sitting there and the Pharisees began to reason, wondering, "Who is this that speaks blasphemies like that? Who can forgive sins but God alone?"

But Jesus, perceiving their thoughts, answered them,

Why do you reason these things in your hearts? Which is easier, to say to the paralytic, *Your sins are forgiven,* or to say, *Arise and take up your bed and walk?* But so that you may know that the Son of Man has authority on earth to forgive sins …

He then said to the paralyzed man,

… I tell you, arise, take up your cot, and go to your house.

The paralytic immediately rose up before them and took the cot that he was lying on and went out – in front of them all – to his house, glorifying God.

When the crowds saw it, they were all amazed and filled with fear, and they too glorified God, who had given such authority to a man.

They said among themselves, "We have seen strange things today. We have never seen anything like this."

Jesus addresses questions of propriety

Jesus went out again by the seaside. The entire crowd came to him, and he taught them.

⁕⊱ᴑⱣ⊰⁕

After this, he went out and, as he passed by from there, Jesus saw a tax collector named Matthew Levi sitting at the tax office.

He said to him, "Follow me." And Matthew rose up, left everything, and followed him.

⁕⊱ᴑⱣ⊰⁕

Later, Matthew made a great feast for him in his house, and many tax collectors and sinners came and reclined with Jesus and his disciples.

When the Pharisees and their scribes saw it, they said to his disciples, "Why does he eat and drink with tax collectors and sinners?"

Jesus heard it and answered them,

> Those who are sick have need for a physician, not those who are healthy. Go and learn what this means, *I desire mercy and not sacrifice,* for I came to call not the righteous, but sinners to repentance.

John's disciples and the Pharisees were fasting, and they came and asked Jesus, "Why do John's disciples, like the disciples of the Pharisees, often fast and pray, but your disciples eat and drink – they do not fast?"

Jesus said to them,

The friends of the bridegroom cannot fast as long as the bridegroom is with them, can they? But the days will come when the bridegroom is taken away from them, and then will they fast in those days.

He also told them a parable,

No one puts a piece of unshrunk cloth on an old garment, for the patch would tear away from the garment – the new from the old – and a worse hole is made.

And no one puts new wine into old wineskins – the new wine will burst the skins and be spilled – the wine pours out and the skins are destroyed. New wine must be put into fresh wineskins so both are preserved. And no one having drunk old wine immediately desires new, for he says, *The old is better.*

Jesus performs on the sabbath

Jesus was going through the grain fields one day, on the sabbath. His disciples were hungry and, as they went, plucked the heads of grain and, rubbing them in their hands, began to eat.

But when some of the Pharisees saw it, they said to him, "Behold, your disciples do what is not lawful to do on the sabbath."

Jesus answered, saying,

Have you not read what David did when he and those with him were hungry? He entered the house of God, when Abiathar was high priest, and ate the show bread, which is not lawful for anyone to eat except for the priests. Then he gave some also to those who were with him.

Or have you not read in the law that on the sabbath day the priests in the temple profane the sabbath and yet are guiltless?

I tell you, one greater than the temple is here. But, if you had known what this means, *I desire mercy and not sacrifice,* you would not have condemned the guiltless, for the Son of Man is lord of the sabbath. The sabbath was made for man, not man for the sabbath.

❧❦❧

He departed and entered into the synagogue and taught, and a man was there with a withered right hand.

The scribes and the Pharisees watched Jesus to see whether he would heal on the sabbath, so that they might find an accusation to use against him.

Though he knew their thoughts, he said to the man who had the withered hand, "Rise up, and stand in the middle."

The Pharisees asked him, "Is it lawful to heal on the sabbath day?"

Jesus arose and stood and said to them,

If you had one sheep and if this one falls into a pit on the sabbath day, who among you will not grab it and lift it out?

And of how much more value then is a man than a sheep?

So is it lawful to do good or to do harm on the sabbath, to save a life or to kill?

While they were silent, he – being grieved at the hardening of their hearts – looked around at them with anger, then said to the man, "Stretch out your hand." The man did, and his hand was restored as sound as the other.

But the Pharisees were filled with rage and immediately conspired with the Herodians on what they might do to destroy Jesus.

Jesus teaches on the mountain

Jesus went up the mountain and stood on a level place, and his disciples and a great crowd of people from all Judea, Jerusalem, and the seacoast of Tyre and Sidon came to hear him and to be healed of their diseases.

They all sought to touch him, for power came out from him and healed them all. Those troubled by unclean spirits were being healed.

When he had sat down, he lifted up his eyes and opened his mouth. Jesus taught them, saying,

Blessed are those who weep, for they will laugh.
Blessed are those who mourn, for they shall be comforted.
Blessed are those who hunger and thirst, for they shall be filled.
Blessed are the merciful, for they shall obtain mercy.
Blessed are the meek, for they shall inherit the earth.

Blessed are the poor in spirit, for theirs is the kingdom of God.
Blessed are the pure in heart, for they shall see God.
Blessed are the peacemakers, for they shall be called children of God.
Blessed are those who have been persecuted for righteousness'
sake, for theirs is the kingdom of heaven.

Blessed are you when people shall hate you, persecute you, exclude and mock you, and throw out your name as evil for the sake of the Son of Man – just as their forebears persecuted the prophets who were before you. So rejoice and be exceedingly glad, for great is your reward in heaven.

But woe to you who are rich, for you have received your consolation. Woe to you who are full now, for you will be hungry. Woe to you who laugh now, for you will mourn and weep. Woe to you when all speak well of you, for their forebears did the same thing to the false prophets.

But I tell you who hear, you are the light of the world, and the eye is the lamp of your body. If therefore your eye is evil, your whole body will be full of darkness. And if the light that is in you is darkness, how great the darkness is. But, if your eye is sound, your whole body will be full of light.

No one lights a lamp and puts it under a measuring basket but puts it instead on a stand, and it shines to all who are in the house. Just so, let your light shine before others, so that they may see your good works and glorify your Father who is in heaven. A city located on a hill cannot be hidden.

You are the salt of the earth. But, if the salt has lost its flavor, with what will it be salted? It is then good for nothing but is to be cast out and trodden under foot. And can the blind guide the blind? Will they not both fall into a pit? Truly I tell you, a disciple is not above his teacher, but everyone fully trained will be like his teacher.

You have heard it said, *An eye for an eye, and a tooth for a tooth.* But I tell you, *Do not resist an evil one.* To anyone who strikes you on your right cheek, turn the other also. With anyone who compels you to go one mile, go two miles. If anyone sues you to take away your coat, let that one have your cloak also.

Give to anyone who asks of you, and do not turn away anyone who desires to borrow from you. If someone takes away your goods, do not ask for them back again. Do exactly so to others as you would like them to do to you.

Again you have heard it said, *You shall not make false vows but shall perform your vows to the Lord,* but I tell you, *Do not swear at all.* Do not swear by heaven, for it is the throne of God, or by the earth, for it is the footstool of his feet, or by Jerusalem, for it is the city of the great king.

Also do not swear by your head, for you cannot make one hair white or black. But let your *Yes* be *Yes* and your *No* be *No.* Anything more than this is of the evil one.

You have heard it said, *You shall not commit adultery,* but I tell you that everyone who gazes at a woman to lust after her has already committed adultery with her in his heart.

If your right eye causes you to stumble, pluck it out and throw it away. If your right hand causes you to stumble, cut it off and throw it away. It is more profitable for you that one of your members should perish, than for your whole body to be cast into hell.

It was also said, *Whoever shall put away his wife, let him give her a writing of divorce,* but I tell you that whoever puts away his wife, except for the cause of sexual immorality, makes her an adulteress, and whoever marries her when she is put away commits adultery.

You have heard it said, *You shall not murder,* and, *Whoever murders shall be in danger of the judgment.* But I tell you that any man who is angry with his brother shall be in danger of the judgment. He who insults his brother shall be in danger of the council, and he who says, *You fool,* shall be in danger of the fire of hell.

Therefore, if you are offering your gift at the altar and there remember that your brother has something against you, leave your gift there before the altar and go your way. First be reconciled to your brother, and then come and offer your gift.

Why do you not judge for yourselves what is right? When you are going before the magistrate with your adversary, try diligently on the way to reach agreement with him, lest he drag you to the judge who delivers you to the officer who throws you into prison. You will by no means get out of there until you have paid your very last lepton.

You have heard it said, *You shall love your neighbor and hate your enemy.* But I tell you, love your enemies, do good to those who hate you, bless those who curse you, and pray for those who mistreat you and persecute you.

If you love those who love you, what reward do you have? Even sinners love those who love them. If you do good to those who do good to you, what more do you do than others? Even sinners do the same. If you lend to those from whom you hope to receive, what credit is that to you? Even sinners lend to sinners, to receive back as much. But love your enemies, do good, and lend, expecting nothing back, and your reward will be great.

You will be children of your Father in heaven, for he is kind toward the evil and unthankful. He makes his sun rise on the good and the evil and sends rain on the just and the unjust.

Be merciful, even as your Father is merciful. Be perfect, just as your Father in heaven is perfect.

❧❧❧

Do not think that I came to destroy the law or the prophets. I did not come to destroy, but to fulfill. Truly I tell you, until heaven and earth pass away, not one small letter, not even one tiny stroke shall pass from the law until all things are accomplished.

Therefore, whoever shall break even the least of these commandments and teach others to do so shall be called least in the kingdom of heaven. But whoever shall do them and teach them shall be called great in the kingdom of heaven. In truth, unless your righteousness exceeds that of the scribes and Pharisees, there is no way you will enter into the kingdom of heaven.

Why do you call me, *Lord, Lord,* and do not do the things I say? Only the one who does the will of my Father will enter into the kingdom of heaven.

On the day of judgment, many will tell me, *Lord, Lord, did we not prophesy in your name, cast out demons in your name, and do many mighty works in your name?*

Then I will tell them, *I never knew you. Depart from me, you who work iniquity.*

Everyone who comes to me, hears my words, and does them is like a wise man building a house, who dug and went deep and laid a foundation on the rock. When the rain came down and a flood arose, the stream broke against that house and the winds blew and beat it, but the house did not fall, for it was founded on the rock.

But the one who hears and does not do is like a foolish man who built a house on the sand without a foundation. When the rain came down and the floods came and the stream broke against that house, immediately it fell, and great was the ruin.

The gate that leads to destruction is wide, the way is broad, and many are those who enter by it. The gate that leads to life is narrow, the way is restricted, and few are those who find it.

Enter by the narrow gate.

And beware of false prophets, who come to you in sheep's clothing but inwardly are ravening wolves. As each tree is known by its own fruit, you will know the false prophets by their fruit.

Do you gather grapes from thorns or figs from thistles? Even so, a good tree cannot produce evil fruit, neither can a corrupt tree produce good fruit, and every tree that does not grow good fruit is cut down and thrown into the fire.

Be careful that you do not do your charitable giving before others in order to be seen by them, or else you have no reward from your Father in heaven. Therefore, when you do merciful deeds, do not sound a trumpet before you as the hypocrites do, in the synagogues and in the streets, so that they may get glory from others. Truly I tell you, they have received their reward.

When you do merciful deeds, do not let your left hand know what your right hand does, so that your merciful deeds may be done in secret. Your Father who sees in secret will reward you openly.

When you fast, do not be like the hypocrites with sad faces. They disfigure their faces, so that they may be seen by others to be fasting. Truly I tell you, they have received their reward.

When you fast, anoint your head and wash your face, so that you are not seen by others to be fasting. Your Father who sees in secret will reward you openly.

And when you pray, do not be like the hypocrites who love to stand and pray in the synagogues and in the corners of the streets, so that they may be seen by others. Truly I tell you, they have received their reward.

When you pray, enter into your inner chamber, shut your door, and pray to your Father in secret. Your Father who sees in secret will reward you openly. When you pray, say,

Our Father in heaven, may your name be kept holy.
May your kingdom come. May your will be done on earth,
as it is in heaven. Give us each day our daily bread.
Forgive us our debts, as we ourselves forgive those indebted to us.
Bring us not into temptation, but deliver us from the evil one.
For yours is the kingdom, the power, and the glory forever.

Do not use vain repetitions as the Gentiles do. They think that they will be heard because of their many words. But your Father knows what things you need before you ask him. Do not be like them.

Also, do not give that which is holy to the dogs, and do not throw your pearls before the pigs. They will trample them under their feet then turn and tear you to pieces.

Do not judge, and you will not be judged. Do not condemn, and you will not be condemned. Set free, and you will be set free. Give, and it will be given to you.

A good measure – pressed down, shaken together, and running over – will be given to you, and the same measure you give will be the measure you get back. If you forgive others their trespasses, your heavenly Father will also forgive you. But, if you do not forgive others their trespasses, your Father will not forgive you either. With whatever judgment you judge, you will be judged.

Why do you see the speck in your brother's eye, but do not consider the beam that is in your own eye? Or how can you say, *Brother, let me remove the speck in your eye,* while that beam is in yours? You hypocrite.

First remove the beam out of your own eye, and then you can see clearly to remove the speck out of your brother's.

The good person brings out that which is good out of the good treasure of the heart, and the evil person brings out that which is evil out of the evil treasure of the heart. The mouth speaks out of the abundance of the heart.

Finally I tell you, do not be anxious about your life or about your body – what you will eat, what you will drink, what you will wear. Life is more than food, and the body is more than clothing.

See the birds of the sky – they do not sow, neither do they reap nor gather into barns. Your heavenly Father feeds them. Are you not of much more value than they? And which of you can add one moment to your lifespan or one cubit to your height by being anxious? If you are not able to do even the least things, why are you anxious about the rest?

Consider the lilies of the field, how they grow – they neither toil nor spin, yet I tell you that even Solomon in all his glory was not dressed like one of these. But, if God so clothes the grass of the field, which today exists and tomorrow is thrown into the oven, how much more will he clothe you, you of little faith?

Do not seek what you will eat or what you will drink, and do not be anxious. The nations of the world seek after all of these things, but your Father knows that you need them. But seek God's kingdom and his righteousness, and all these things will be given to you as well.

Therefore do not be anxious for tomorrow, for tomorrow will be anxious for itself. Each day's own evil is sufficient.

Imagine that you go to a friend at midnight and tell him, *Friend, lend me three loaves of bread, for a friend of mine has come to me from a journey, and I have nothing to set before him.* And he answers from within, *Do not bother me. The door is now shut, and my children are with me in bed. I cannot get up and give it to you.*

Although he says he will not rise and give it to you, because he is your friend and because of your persistence, he will get up and give as many as you need.

Which of you, if your son asks for bread, will give him a stone? or, if he asks for a fish, will give him a snake instead? or, if he asks for an egg, will give him a scorpion? If you then, being evil, know how to give good gifts to your children, how much more will your heavenly Father give good things to those who ask him?

I tell you, *Ask, and it will be given you. Seek, and you will find. Knock, and it will be opened for you.* Everyone who asks receives. Everyone who seeks finds. For everyone who knocks it will be opened.

Do not be afraid, little flock, for it is your Father's good pleasure to give you the kingdom. But no one can serve two masters, for you either will hate the one and love the other or else be devoted to one and despise the other. You cannot serve both God and wealth.

Sell what you have, and give gifts to the needy. Do not lay up treasures for yourselves on the earth, where moth and rust consume, and where thieves break through and steal.

Make purses for yourselves that do not grow old – a treasure that does not fail in the heavens, where neither moth nor rust consumes and where no thief approaches.

Where your treasure is, there your heart will be also.

When Jesus finished saying these things, the crowds were astonished at his teaching, for he taught them not like the scribes, but as one with authority.

Jesus acknowledges the faithful

After he had finished speaking in the hearing of the people, Jesus came down from the mountain, and great crowds followed him.

※ั๊ช๊ฬ※

He entered into Capernaum.

A centurion there had a dear servant, who was sick and at the point of death. When he heard about Jesus, he sent elders of the Jews to him, to ask him to come and save his servant.

When they came to Jesus, they begged him earnestly, saying, "The centurion is worthy for you to do this for him, for he loves our nation, and he built our synagogue for us. His servant lies in the house paralyzed, grievously tormented."

Jesus said, "I will come and heal him."

※ั๊ช๊ฬ※

Jesus went with them. When he was not far from the house, the centurion said to him, "Lord, do not trouble yourself, for I am not worthy for you to come under my roof. But say the word, and my servant will be healed. For I also am a man under authority, having soldiers under me. I tell this one, 'Go,' and he goes, and to another, 'Come,' and he comes, and to my servant, 'Do this,' and he does it."

When Jesus heard this, he marveled at him, and said to those who followed,

Truly I tell you, I have not found such great faith, not even in Israel.

I tell you, many will come from the east and the west and will sit down with Abraham, Isaac, and Jacob in the kingdom of heaven, but the children of the kingdom will be thrown out into the outer darkness. There will be weeping and gnashing of teeth.

Jesus said to the centurion, "Go your way. Let it be done for you as you have believed." His servant was healed in that hour.

⁕ᘛᘚ⁕

Soon afterwards, Jesus went to a city called Nain. Many of his disciples, along with a great crowd, went with him. When he drew near to the gate of the city, behold, one who was dead was carried out – the only son of his mother, and she was a widow. Many people of the city were with her.

When the Lord saw her, he had compassion on her and said to her, "Do not cry."

He came near and touched the coffin, and the bearers stood still. He said, "Young man, I tell you, arise."

He who was dead sat up and began to speak, and Jesus gave him to his mother. Fear took hold of all, and they glorified God, saying, "A great prophet has arisen among us. God has visited his people."

This report went out concerning him in all of the surrounding region.

⁕ᘛᘚ⁕

A Pharisee named Simon invited Jesus to eat with him. Jesus entered into the Pharisee's house and sat at the table.

Behold, a woman in the city who was a sinner – when she knew that he was reclining in the Pharisee's house, she brought an alabaster jar of ointment. Standing behind Jesus, weeping, she began to wet his feet with her tears, and she wiped them with the hair of her head, kissed his feet, and anointed them with the ointment.

When the Pharisee who had invited him saw it, he said to himself, "This man, if he were a prophet, would have perceived who and what kind of woman this is who touches him – that she is a sinner."

Jesus answered him, "Simon, I have something to tell you."

He said, "Teacher, say on."

Jesus said, "A certain lender had two debtors. The one owed five hundred denarii, and the other fifty. When they could not pay, he forgave them both. Which of them therefore will love him most?"

Simon answered, "He, I suppose, to whom he forgave the most."

He said to him, "You have judged correctly."

Turning to the woman, he said to Simon, "Do you see this woman? I entered your house, and you gave me no water for my feet. But she has wet my feet with her tears and wiped them with the hair of her head. You gave me no kiss but she, since the time I came in, has not ceased to kiss my feet. You did not anoint my head with oil, but she has anointed my feet with ointment. Therefore I tell you, her sins, which are many, are forgiven, for she loved much. But to whom little is forgiven, the same loves little."

He said to her, "Your sins are forgiven."

Those who sat at the table with him began to say to themselves, "Who is this who even forgives sins?"

He said to the woman, "Your faith has saved you. Go in peace."

~~❧~~

Soon afterwards, he continued to go through cities and villages, proclaiming and bringing the good news of the kingdom of God.

Part 5

ITINERANT MINISTRY

ITINERANT MINISTRY

An account of events related to
the itinerant ministry of Jesus the Messiah

Part 5

Jesus traverses the Sea of Galilee

PERCEIVING THAT THE PHARISEES conspired against him, Jesus withdrew with his disciples to the sea.

A great multitude from Galilee followed him. Hearing what great things he did, people came to him from Judea, Jerusalem, Idumaea, beyond the Jordan, and from around Tyre and Sidon.

He had healed many, so those who had diseases tried to get close so that they might touch him. Because of the crowd, he asked his disciples to have a boat near him so that they would not press on him.

Whenever the unclean spirits saw him, they fell down before him and cried, "You are the Son of God." He sternly warned that they should not make him known.

※⟨ℰⅉ⟩※

As they went on the way, a scribe came and said to him, "Teacher, I will follow you wherever you go."

Jesus said to him,

The foxes have holes, and the birds of the sky have nests, but the Son of Man has nowhere to lay his head.

※⟨ℰⅉ⟩※

Jesus said, "Follow me," to one of his disciples, who replied, "Lord, allow me first to go and bury my father."

But Jesus said to him,

Follow me, and leave the dead to bury their own dead. You go and announce the kingdom of God.

Another said, "I want to follow you, Lord, but first allow me to bid farewell to those who are at my house."

Jesus said to him,

No one who put his hand to the plow and looks back is fit for the kingdom of God.

⁕⟿⟾⁕

One day, when evening had come, Jesus saw the great crowds around him and he ordered, "Let us go over to the other side." Leaving the crowd, he got into a boat just as he was, and his disciples followed him. Then they launched out, and other boats were with them.

As they sailed, Jesus fell asleep.

⁕⟿⟾⁕

A violent windstorm arose, so much that the boat was soon covered with the waves, and they believed they were taking on dangerous amounts of water. But Jesus was in the stern, asleep on the cushion.

They came to him and woke him, saying, "Master, save us. We are dying."

He said to them, "Why are you afraid, you of little faith?"

Then he got up, rebuked the wind and said to the raging water, "Peace. Be still."

The wind ceased, and there was a great calm.

He said to them, "How is it that you have no faith?"

Being afraid, they marveled and said to one another, "What kind of man is this, that he commands the winds and the water, and even they obey him?"

Jesus banishes unclean spirits

They arrived at the other side, to the country of the Gergesenes, which is opposite Galilee.

When Jesus stepped out of the boat on to shore, a certain man of the city who had demons for a long time met him.

※

The man lived in the tombs, and he wore no clothes.

He was exceedingly fierce, so much so that nobody could pass that way, and nobody could bind him any more, not even with chains. He had often been kept under guard and bound with fetters and chains, and he tore apart the chains and broke the fetters in pieces.

Nobody had the strength to tame him. Always, night and day, he was crying out in the tombs and in the mountains, and cutting himself with stones.

※

When he saw Jesus from afar, he ran and bowed down to him.

Jesus commanded the unclean spirit to come out of the man, saying, "Come out of the man, you unclean spirit."

The man cried out with a loud voice, "What have I to do with you, Jesus, you Son of the Most High God? I beg you by God, do not torment me."

Jesus asked him, "What is your name?"

He said to him, "My name is Legion, for we are many." The demons in him begged Jesus not to command them out of the country and into the abyss.

※ᘛᘚ※

Now a herd of many pigs was there feeding on the mountain, and all the demons begged him, "If you cast us out, permit us to go away into the herd of pigs."

Jesus gave them permission at once. He said to them, "Go."

The unclean spirits came out and entered into the pigs and, behold, the whole herd of pigs, of about two thousand, rushed down the steep bank into the sea and drowned.

※ᘛᘚ※

Those who fed them saw what had happened, and they fled, telling everything – including what happened to those possessed with demons – to people in the city and in the country.

※ᘛᘚ※

The entire city came out to see what had happened.

When they came to Jesus, they found the man from whom the demons had gone out sitting at Jesus' feet, clothed and in his right mind – the very man who had the legion.

Those who saw it spoke about how he who had been possessed by demons was healed and about the pigs, and all the people were very much afraid.

They begged Jesus to depart from their region.

※❀❀

As Jesus was getting into the boat, he who had been possessed by demons begged that he might go with him. But Jesus did not allow this and sent him away, saying, "Go to your house, to your friends, and tell them what great things the Lord has done for you and how he had mercy on you."

He went his way, proclaiming throughout the cities in Decapolis what great things Jesus had done for him, and everyone marveled.

※❀❀

And Jesus entered the boat and crossed over the water and came into his own city.

Jesus rescues the afflicted

When Jesus returned by boat to the other side, a great crowd was waiting for him. They welcomed him and gathered to him by the sea.

Behold, a ruler of the synagogue, named Jairus, came to him. And, seeing Jesus, he fell at his feet and begged him to come to his house, saying, "My little daughter is at the point of death. Come and lay your hand on her, so that she may be made healthy and live." She was his only daughter, about twelve years of age.

Jesus got up and followed him, as did his disciples. As he went, a great crowd followed him, and they pressed against him on all sides.

⁂

A certain woman, who had an issue of blood for twelve years, had suffered many things by many physicians. She had spent all that she had, but could not be healed by any. She was no better, but rather grew worse.

Having heard the things concerning Jesus, she came up behind him in the crowd and touched the fringe of his cloak, for she said to herself, "If I just touch his garment, I will be made well." Immediately, the flow of her blood stopped, and she felt that she was healed of her affliction.

⁂

Perceiving that the power had gone out from him, Jesus turned around in the crowd and asked, "Who touched me?"

His disciples said to him, "Master, the crowds press and jostle you, and yet you say, 'Who touched me?'"

But Jesus said, "Someone did touch me." He looked around to see who had done this thing. But the woman, who saw that she was not hidden, came fearing and trembling and falling down before him. She declared to him, in the presence of all, the reason why she had touched him and how she was healed immediately.

He said to her, "Daughter, your faith has made you well. Go in peace and be cured of your disease." And the woman was made well from that hour.

⁂

While Jesus still spoke, one from the synagogue ruler's house came to say, "Your daughter is dead. Do not trouble the teacher any more."

But hearing this, Jesus said to the ruler of the synagogue, "Do not be afraid. Only believe, and she will be healed."

❈

He allowed no one to follow him except Simon, James, and John, the brother of James. When they came to the synagogue ruler's house, Jesus saw flute players and the crowd in an uproar – with noisy disorder of weeping and great wailing.

He said to them, "Why do you make an uproar and weep? The child is not dead, but is sleeping."

Knowing that she was dead, they ridiculed him.

❈

But he put them all outside. Then he took the father of the child, her mother, and those who were with him, and went in where the child was.

Taking the child by the hand, he said to her, "Talitha cum" – which means, "Girl, get up." Immediately, the girl's spirit returned, and she rose up and walked. Then he commanded that something be given to her to eat.

Her parents were greatly amazed, but he strictly ordered them to tell no one what had been done.

❈

Yet the report of this went out into all that land.

＊ﾞﾞﾞ＊

As Jesus passed from there, two blind men followed him, calling out, "Have mercy on us, son of David."

When he entered the house, the blind men came to him. Jesus said to them, "Do you believe that I am able to do this?"

They told him, "Yes, Lord."

Then he touched their eyes, saying, "According to your faith let it be done to you." And their eyes were opened.

Jesus strictly commanded them, "See that no one knows about this."

But they went out and spread his fame abroad in all that land.

＊ﾞﾞﾞ＊

As they went out, a mute man who was demon possessed was brought to him.

When Jesus cast out the demon, the mute man spoke. The crowds marveled, saying, "Nothing like this has ever been seen in Israel."

＊ﾞﾞﾞ＊

At that time, Jesus said,

> I thank you, Father, Lord of heaven and earth, that you hid these things from the wise and understanding and revealed them to infants. Yes, Father, for so it was well-pleasing in your sight.

> All things have been delivered to me by my Father. No one knows the Son except the Father, neither does anyone know the Father except the Son and anyone to whom the Son desires to reveal him.

**Come to me – all of you who labor and are heavily burdened –
and I will give you rest. Take my yoke upon you and learn from
me, for I am gentle and lowly in heart, and you will find rest for
your souls. For my yoke is easy, and my burden is light.**

⁕ᴗᴗᴗ⁕

While he was yet speaking to the crowds, behold, his mother
and his brothers came to him, but they could not get near him.
Standing outside, seeking to speak to him, they sent to him and
called him.

He was told by some, "Your mother and your brothers stand
outside, looking for you and desiring to speak to you."

He answered, "Who are my mother and my brothers?" Looking at those who sat around him, he stretched out his hand towards
his disciples and said,

Behold my mother and my brothers.

**Whoever hears the word of God and does the will of my Father in
heaven, that person is my brother and sister and mother.**

⁕ᴗᴗᴗ⁕

He went from there and came to his own country, and his
disciples followed him.

When the sabbath came, he began to teach in the synagogue,
and many hearing him were astonished.

They said, "Where did this man get these things – the
wisdom that is given him and these mighty works that have come
about by his hands? Is this not the carpenter's son? Is not his
mother called Mary, and his brothers, James, Joses, Simon, and

Judas? Are not all of his sisters with us? Where then did this man get all of these things?" They were offended by him.

But Jesus said to them, "A prophet is not without honor, except in his own country, among his own relatives, and in his own house." And he did not do many mighty works there, except that he laid his hands on a few sick people and healed them. And he marveled because of their unbelief.

Jesus charges the chosen ones

It happened in these days that Jesus went to the mountain to pray, and he continued all night in prayer to God. When it was day, he called his disciples, and they went to him. He chose twelve as apostles, that they might be with him and that he might send them out to proclaim. He gave them power and authority to cast out unclean spirits and to heal every disease and sickness.

These are the twelve —

- Simon, whom he named Cephas, and his brother, Andrew
- James and John, sons of Zebedee, whom he surnamed Boanerges, which means Sons of Thunder
- Philip and Bartholomew,
- Matthew, the tax collector, and Thomas, who was called Didymus
- James, son of Alphaeus, and Thaddaeus — also called Judas, son of James
- Simon the Canaanite, who was called the Zealot, and
- Judas Iscariot, who betrayed him.

Jesus sent them forth to heal the sick and to proclaim the kingdom of God. He commanded them to wear sandals but to take nothing else for their journey – no staff, no bag, no bread, no money in their belts, not even an extra tunic. He said, "The laborer is worthy of his food."

Then Jesus said to them,

The harvest is indeed plentiful, but the laborers are few. Pray therefore that the Lord of the harvest will send out laborers into his harvest.

Do not go among the Gentiles, and do not enter into any city of the Samaritans. Rather, go to the lost sheep of the house of Israel. As you go, heal the sick, cleanse the lepers, cast out demons, and proclaim, saying, *The kingdom of heaven is at hand.* Freely you received, so freely give.

Into whatever city or village you enter, find out who in it is worthy, and stay there until you depart. As you enter into the household, greet it. If the household is worthy, let your peace come on it but, if it is not worthy, let your peace return to you.

As many as do not receive you nor hear your words, shake off even the dust from your feet as you leave, as a testimony against them. Truly I tell you, it will be more tolerable for the land of Sodom and Gomorrah in the day of judgment than for that city.

Whoever receives a prophet in the name of a prophet will receive a prophet's reward. Whoever receives a righteous person in the name of a righteous person will receive a righteous person's reward. Whoever gives one of these little ones just a cup of cold water to drink in the name of a disciple – truly I tell you, none of these will in any way lose the reward.

Whoever receives you receives me, and whoever receives me and confesses me before others receives him who sent me. I will also confess before my Father in heaven.

But whoever denies me before others, I will deny before my Father in heaven. And whoever loves father or mother, son or daughter more than me is not worthy of me. Whoever does not take the cross and follow after me is also not worthy of me. Those who seek life will lose it, and those who lose life for my sake will find it.

Do not think that I came to send peace on the earth. I did not come to send peace. I came to throw fire on the earth. I wish it were already kindled. But I have a baptism to be baptized with, and how distressed I am until it is accomplished.

I have come to bring division and a sword. I came to divide – to set against each other a son and his father, a daughter and her mother, a daughter-in-law and her mother-in-law.

A man's foes will be those of his own household – brother will deliver up brother to death, and the father his child. Children will rise up against parents and cause them to be put to death.

You will be hated by all for my name's sake, but he who endures to the end will be saved.

Behold, I send you out as sheep in the midst of wolves. Therefore be wise as serpents and harmless as doves. And, when they persecute you in this city, flee into the next. Truly I tell you, you will not have gone through the cities of Israel until the Son of Man has come.

A disciple is not above his teacher, nor is a servant above his master. It is enough for the disciple that he be like his teacher, and the servant like his master. If they have called the master of the house *Beelzebul,* how much more they will call those of his household.

Therefore do not be afraid of them. Fear those who are able to destroy both soul and body in hell, but do not be afraid of those who kill the body but are not able to kill the soul. Nothing is covered that will not be revealed, and nothing is hidden that will not be known.

What I tell you in the darkness, speak in the light, and what you hear whispered in the ear, proclaim on the housetops.

When Jesus had finished directing his twelve apostles, he began to send them out two by two.

They departed and went throughout the villages, proclaiming the good news and declaring that people should repent. They cast out many demons and anointed many with oil who were sick, and they healed everywhere.

Jesus also departed from there to teach and proclaim in their cities. The report about him went throughout the region, and great crowds – from Galilee, Syria, the Decapolis, Jerusalem, Judea, and from beyond the Jordan – followed him.

They brought to him all who were sick – including epileptics, paralytics, and those afflicted with various diseases and torments or possessed with demons – and he healed them.

Part 6

GALILEAN
TEACHING

GALILEAN TEACHING

An account of events related to
the teaching in Galilee of Jesus the Messiah

Part 6

The apostles of Jesus return

WHEN THEY HAD RETURNED, the apostles gathered with Jesus and they told him all the things that they had done and taught.

He said to them, "You come to a deserted place and rest awhile," for there were many coming and going, and they had no leisure even to eat. They went away in the boat to a deserted place by themselves.

But the crowds saw them going and many recognized him and followed. Running there on foot from all the cities, a great many arrived before them.

Jesus went out and saw the multitude. He welcomed them and spoke to them of the kingdom of God, and he cured those who needed healing.

Jesus teaches in parables

Jesus sat by the seaside and began to teach. Such a multitude of people from every city came to him that he entered a boat and sat, and all the crowd stood on the beach. He said many things to them in parables. He told them in his teaching,

Listen.

The farmer went out to sow his seed. As he sowed, some seeds fell along the road, and the birds came and devoured them.

Other seeds fell on rocky ground – where they did not have much soil – and immediately they sprang up, because they had no depth of earth. When the sun rose, they were scorched and, because they had no root, they withered away.

Other seeds fell among thorns, which grew up and choked them, and they yielded no fruit. But other seeds fell into the good ground and, when they grew and increased, they yielded fruit some thirty, some sixty, and some one hundred times as much.

As he said these things, he called out,

Let anyone hear who has ears to hear.

※§∅⁋※

He said to them,

If you do not understand this parable, how will you understand all of the parables? Hear then, the parable is this –

The seed is the word of God, and the farmer sows the word.

Those along the road where the word is sown are those who hear. But, when they hear the word of the kingdom and do not understand it, the devil immediately comes and snatches away that which has been sown in their hearts, so that they may not believe and be saved.

Those on the rocky places are the ones who, when they hear the word, immediately receive it with joy. They have no root in themselves, but are short-lived – in time of temptation, when oppression or persecution arises because of the word, immediately they stumble.

Those sown among the thorns are the ones who hear the word but, as they go on their way, are choked with the cares of this age and the deceitfulness of riches, and they bring no fruit to maturity.

Those in the good ground – these are the ones who, when they hear the word, they understand and accept it. They hold it tightly in an honest and good heart and bear fruit with patience – thirty, sixty, and some one hundred times.

※ЖЖ※

He said to them,

No one, having lit a lamp, covers it with a container or under a basket, or puts it under a bed or in a cellar. The lamp is put on a stand, so that those who enter in may see the light. Nothing is hidden that will not be revealed, and nothing is secret that will not be known and come to light.

The eye is the lamp of the body. When your eye is good, your whole body is full of light but, when it is evil, your body is full of darkness.

Therefore, see whether the light in you is darkness. If your whole body is full of light, having no part dark, it will be wholly full of light, as when the lamp gives you light with its bright shining.

Let anyone hear who has ears to hear, and take heed of what you hear. With whatever measure you give, it will be given to you in return, and even more will be given.

It will be given to those who have, and they will have abundance. From those who do not have, even that which they think they have will be taken away.

※ЖЖ※

He said, "What is the kingdom of heaven like? With what shall I compare it?" Jesus spoke the word to them in parables – without a parable, he did not speak.

※ЖЖ※

The kingdom of heaven is like a grain of mustard seed that someone took and sowed in the garden. A mustard seed is smaller than all seeds but, when it is sown in the earth, it becomes greater than all the herbs. It puts out great branches and becomes a tree, so that the birds of the air come and lodge in its branches.

※ЖЖ※

The kingdom of heaven is like yeast which a woman took and blended in three measures of flour until it was all leavened.

※⚜※

The kingdom of heaven is like a treasure hidden in the field, which a man found and hid again. In his joy, he went and sold all that he had and bought that field.

※⚜※

The kingdom of heaven is like a merchant seeking fine pearls. Having found one pearl of great price, he went and sold all that he had and bought it.

※⚜※

The kingdom of heaven is like a dragnet that was cast into the sea and gathered some fish of every kind. When it was filled, the fishermen drew it up on the beach. They sat down and gathered the good into containers but threw away the bad.

So it will be in the end of the world – the angels will come forth and separate the wicked from among the righteous and cast them into the furnace of fire. There will be weeping and gnashing of teeth.

※⚜※

He set before them another parable,

The kingdom of heaven is like a man who sowed good seed in his field. But after, while people slept, his enemy came and sowed darnel weeds among the wheat and went away.

The seed sprung up and grew – though no one knew how – and the earth brought forth fruit, first the blade, then the ear, then the full grain in the ear. But when the blade sprang up, the darnel weeds appeared also.

The servants of the householder came and said to him, *Sir, where did this darnel come from? Did you not sow good seed in your field?* He said to them, *An enemy has done this.*

The servants asked, *Do you want us to go and gather the weeds?*

But he said, *No, lest perhaps, while you gather up the darnel weeds, you root up the wheat with them. Let both grow together until the harvest, and in the harvest time – when the fruit is ripe – I will tell the reapers, as they put forth the sickles, 'Gather up the darnel weeds first and bind them in bundles to burn them, but gather the wheat into my barn.'*

Let anyone hear who has ears to hear.

꿍

When Jesus had finished these parables, he departed from there and went into the house.

꿍

When he was alone, the twelve disciples who were around him asked, "Why do you speak to them in parables?"

He said to them,

You are given to know the mysteries of the kingdom of God, but it is not given to those who are outside. I speak to them in parables, so that seeing they may not see, and hearing they may not hear or understand.

In them the prophecy of Isaiah is fulfilled, which says, *By hearing you will hear and will in no way understand, seeing you will see and will in no way perceive, lest perhaps they turn again and their sins be forgiven –* for this people's heart has grown callous, their ears are dull of hearing, they have closed their eyes. But blessed are your eyes, for they see, and your ears, for they hear.

Truly I tell you, many prophets and righteous men desired to see the things which you see and did not see them, to hear the things which you hear and did not hear them.

꿍

He explained everything privately to his disciples. So when his disciples asked him about the parable of the darnel weeds of the field, he explained what this parable meant.

He who sows the good seed is the Son of Man. The field is the world, and the good seed are the children of the kingdom. The darnel weeds are the children of the evil one, and the enemy who sowed them is the devil. The harvest is the end of the age, and the reapers are angels. As the darnel weeds are gathered up and burned with fire, so will it be at the end of this age.

The Son of Man will send out his angels, and they will gather all things that cause stumbling out of his kingdom and those who do iniquity and will cast them into the furnace of fire.

There will be weeping and gnashing of teeth. Then the righteous will shine forth like the sun in the kingdom of their Father.

※◊※

Jesus said to them, "Have you understood all these things?"

They answered him, "Yes." And he said to them,

Therefore every scribe who has been made a disciple in the kingdom of heaven is like a householder who brings out of his treasure new and old things.

Jesus challenges the crowd

The multitude came together again – it was so crowded that they could not even eat bread.

From the crowd, some brought to him one possessed by a demon, and he was mute. Jesus cast out the demon and, when the demon was gone, the mute man spoke.

All the crowds were amazed and said, "Can this be the son of David?"

But some of them said, "He is insane," and the Pharisees said, "This man does not cast out demons except by Beelzebul, the prince of the demons."

Knowing their thoughts, Jesus summoned them and said to them in parables,

You say that I cast out demons by Beelzebul. But, if I cast out demons by Beelzebul, how can Satan cast out Satan?

Every kingdom divided against itself is brought to desolation. The divided kingdom cannot stand – the house falls against itself. Every city or house divided against itself will not stand.

When the strong man, fully armed, guards his house, his goods are safe. But when someone stronger attacks and overcomes him, he takes the armor in which the man trusted. After the strong man is first bound, then the attacker will plunder his house.

Therefore, if Satan casts out Satan, he has risen up against himself and is divided. How then will his kingdom stand? Satan cannot stand – he has but an end.

If I cast out demons by Beelzebul, by whom do your children cast them out? They will be your judges. But, if I cast out demons by the Spirit of God, then the kingdom of God has come upon you.

Truly I tell you, every sin and blasphemy will be forgiven, but blasphemy against the Holy Spirit will not be forgiven. Everyone who speaks a word against the Son of Man will be forgiven, but whoever blasphemes against the Holy Spirit is guilty of an eternal sin and will never be forgiven, either in this age or in the age to come.

The good person brings good things out of good treasure, and the evil one brings evil things out of evil treasure.

So you offspring of vipers, how can you – being evil – speak good things? Either make the tree good and its fruit good, or make the tree corrupt and its fruit corrupt. The tree is known by its fruit, and the mouth speaks out of the abundance of the heart.

Truly I tell you, on the day of judgment, people will need to account for every idle word spoken. By your words you will be justified, and by your words you will be condemned.

Whoever is not with me is against me, and whoever does not gather with me scatters.

As he said these things, a certain woman out of the crowd lifted up her voice and said to him, "Blessed is the womb that bore you and the breasts which nursed you."

But he said, "On the contrary, blessed are those who hear the word of God and keep it."

While the multitudes were gathering together to him, certain of the scribes and Pharisees said, "Teacher, we want to see a sign from you."

He answered them,

This is an evil and adulterous generation, and it seeks after a sign. No sign will be given to it but the sign of the prophet Jonah – even as Jonah became a sign to the Ninevites, so will the Son of Man be to this generation. As Jonah was three days and three nights in the belly of the whale, so will the Son of Man be three days and three nights in the heart of the earth.

The people of Nineveh will stand up in the judgment and condemn this generation, for they repented at the proclaiming of Jonah and, behold, one greater than Jonah is here.

The Queen of the South will rise up in the judgment and condemn this generation, for she came from the ends of the earth to hear the wisdom of Solomon and, behold, someone greater than Solomon is here.

܀

When the unclean spirit has gone out of a person, it passes through waterless places seeking rest and, finding none, it says, *I will turn back to the house from which I came.*

When it returns, it finds it empty, swept, and put in order. Then it goes and takes seven other spirits more evil than itself.

They enter in and dwell there, and the last state of that person becomes worse than the first.

Even so it will be also with this evil generation.

Jesus confers woe on hypocrites

As he spoke, a certain Pharisee asked him to dine with him. Jesus went in and sat at the table. The Pharisee marveled that he had not first washed himself before dinner.

Jesus said to him,

Now you Pharisees cleanse the outside of the cup and of the platter, but your inward part is full of extortion and wickedness.

You fools, did not the one who made the outside make the inside also? But give for gifts to the needy those things that are within and, behold, all things will be clean to you.

But woe to you, Pharisees, for you tithe mint and rue and every herb, but you bypass justice and the love of God. You ought to have done these but ought not to have left the other undone.

Woe to you, Pharisees, for you love the best seats in the synagogues and the greetings in the marketplaces.

Woe to you, Pharisees, for you are like hidden graves, and the men who walk over them do not know it.

꙳ᴗꙮᴗ꙳

One of the lawyers there said, "Teacher, in saying this you insult us also."

And Jesus said,

Woe also to you, lawyers, for you load people with burdens that are difficult to carry, and you yourselves will not even lift one finger to help carry those burdens.

Woe to you, lawyers, for you took away the key of knowledge. You did not enter in yourselves, and you hindered those who were entering in.

Woe to you, lawyers, for you build the tombs of the prophets, and your ancestors killed them. So you testify and consent to the works of your ancestors – for they killed the prophets, and you build their tombs.

The wisdom of God said, *I will send to them prophets and apostles, and they will kill and persecute some of them,* so that the blood of all the prophets – shed from the foundation of the world – may be required of this generation, from the blood of Abel to the blood of Zachariah, who perished between the altar and the sanctuary.

Truly I tell you, it will be required of this generation.

As he said these things to them, the scribes and the Pharisees began to be terribly angry, to draw many things out of him, and to lie in wait for him, seeking to catch him in something he might say, so that they might accuse him.

Jesus speaks of getting ready

Meanwhile, a crowd of many thousands gathered together, so many that they trampled on each other. He began to speak, first to his disciples,

Beware of the yeast of the Pharisees, which is hypocrisy.

There is nothing covered up that will not be revealed, nor anything hidden that will not be known. Therefore, whatever you have said in the darkness will be heard in the light, and what you have spoken in the inner chambers will be proclaimed on the housetops.

When they bring you before the synagogues, the rulers, and the authorities, do not be anxious about how or what you will answer or what you will say, for the Holy Spirit will teach you in that same hour what you must say.

I tell you, my friends, do not be afraid of those who kill the body – after that, there is no more that they can do. But I warn you, fear him who, after he has killed, has power to cast into hell. Yes, I tell you, fear him.

Are not five sparrows sold for two assaria coins? Yet not one of them falls to the ground forgotten by God. Therefore, do not be afraid, for you are of more value than many sparrows. The very hairs of your head are all numbered.

Truly I tell you, everyone who confesses me before others will be confessed by the Son of Man before the angels of God. But whoever denies me in the presence of others will be denied in the presence of the angels of God.

༠༢༠

One in the crowd called to him, "Teacher, tell my brother to divide the inheritance with me."

Jesus said to him, "Who made me a judge or an arbitrator over you?" Then he said, "Beware. Keep yourselves from covetousness, for one's life does not consist of the abundance of the things possessed."

He told them a parable,

The ground of a certain rich man brought forth abundantly. He reasoned within himself, *What will I do, because I do not have room to store my crops?*

Then he said, *This is what I will do. I will pull down my barns and build bigger ones, and there I will store all my grain and my goods. I will tell my soul, 'Soul, you have many goods laid up for many years. Take your ease – eat, drink, be merry.'*

But God said to him, *You foolish one, tonight your soul is required of you. And the things which you have prepared – whose will they be?*

So he who lays up treasure for himself is not rich before God.

※》⊙《※

Let your waist be girded and keep your lamps burning.

Be like those watching for their master when he returns from the marriage feast, so that they may immediately open the door to him when he comes and knocks.

Blessed are those servants who will be watching when the master comes. Truly I tell you, he will dress himself and make them recline and will come and serve them.

If he comes in the second or third watch and finds them so, they will be blessed.

Be ready also, for the Son of Man is coming in an hour that you do not expect him.

Jesus teaches in cities and villages

The twelve apostles were with him, along with certain women who had been healed of evil spirits and infirmities, including Mary who was called Magdalene – from whom seven demons had gone out – and Joanna – the wife of Herod's steward, Chuzas – and Susanna and many others who served him from their possessions.

As he went about through cities and villages, a great crowd was also now going with him. He turned and said to them,

Whoever comes to me and does not hate his own father, mother, wife, children, brothers, and sisters – and, yes, even life also – cannot be my disciple.

Whoever does not bear the cross and come after me cannot be my disciple.

Which of you is like the one who, desiring to build a tower, does not first sit down and count the cost to see if there is enough to complete it?

If he does not, when he has laid a foundation and is not able to finish, everyone who sees begins to mock him, saying, *This man began to build and was not able to finish.*

Or what king, as he goes to encounter another king in war, will not sit down first and consider whether he is able with ten thousand to meet the one who comes against him with twenty thousand?

If he cannot, he sends an envoy while the other is yet a great way off and asks for conditions of peace.

Therefore, whoever of you who does not renounce all that you have cannot be my disciple.

Let anyone hear who has ears to hear.

Now all the tax collectors and sinners were coming close to him to hear him. The Pharisees and the scribes murmured, saying, "This man welcomes sinners and eats with them."

He told them this parable,

Which of you is not like the shepherd who has one hundred sheep, and one of them goes astray. Does he not leave the ninety-nine in the wilderness and seek that which was lost, until he finds it?

When he finds it, truly I tell you, he carries it on his shoulders and rejoices over it more than the ninety-nine which have not gone astray. When he comes home, he calls together his friends and his neighbors, saying to them, *Rejoice with me, for I have found my sheep that was lost.*

See that you do not despise one of these little ones, for I tell you that in heaven their angels always see the face of my Father.

I tell you, it is not the will of your Father in heaven that one of these little ones should perish – for the Son of Man came to save that which was lost. There will be more joy in heaven over one sinner who repents than over ninety-nine righteous people who need no repentance.

Or what woman who had ten drachma coins, if she lost one of them, would not light a lamp, sweep the house, and seek diligently until she found it?

When she finds it, she calls together her friends and neighbors, saying, *Rejoice with me, for I have found the drachma that I had lost.*

Even so, I tell you, there is joy in the presence of the angels of God over one sinner repenting.

Then Jesus said,

A certain man had two sons.

The younger of them said to his father, *Father, give me my share of your property.* So the man divided his livelihood between them.

Not many days after, the younger son gathered all he had together and traveled into a far country. There he wasted his property with riotous living.

When he had spent all of it, a severe famine arose in that country, and he began to be in need. He went and joined up with one of the citizens of that country, who sent him into his fields to feed pigs.

He wanted to fill his belly with the husks that the pigs ate, but no one gave him any. But when he came to himself, he said, *How many of my father's hired servants have bread enough to spare, and I am dying with hunger. I will get up and go to my father and will tell him, 'Father, I have sinned against heaven and in your sight. I am no longer worthy to be called your son. Make me as one of your hired servants.'*

He arose and came to his father.

But while he was still far off, his father saw him and, moved with compassion, he ran and hugged him and kissed him. The son said to him, *Father, I have sinned against heaven and in your sight. I am no longer worthy to be called your son.*

But the father said to his servants, *Bring out the best robe, and put it on him. Put a ring on his hand and shoes on his feet. Bring the fattened calf, kill it, and let us eat and celebrate, for this is my son, who was dead and is alive again. He was lost and is now found.* They began to celebrate.

Now his elder son was in the field. As he came near to the house, he heard music and dancing.

He called one of the servants to him and asked what was going on. The servant said to him, *Your brother has come, and your father has killed the fattened calf, because he has received him back safe and healthy.*

The elder son was angry and would not go in.

His father came out and begged him. But he answered his father, *Behold, I have served you these many years, and I never disobeyed a commandment of yours. But you never gave me a goat, so that I might celebrate with my friends. But when this, your son, came – who has devoured your living with prostitutes – you killed the fattened calf for him.*

The father said to him, *Son, you are always with me, and all that is mine is yours. But it was appropriate to celebrate and be glad, for this, your brother, was dead and is alive again. He was lost and is now found.*

Jesus eschews wealth

Jesus said to his disciples,

There was a certain rich man who had a manager. An accusation had been brought that this man was wasting his possessions. He called the manager and said to him, *What is this that I hear about you? Give an accounting of your management, for you can no longer be manager.*

The manager said to himself, *What will I do, seeing that my lord is taking away the management position from me? I do not have strength to dig. I am ashamed to beg. I know what I will do – so that, when I am removed from management, people may receive me into their houses.*

Calling each one of his lord's debtors to him, he said to the first, *How much do you owe to my lord?* The debtor answered, *A hundred batos of oil.* He said to him, *Take your bill, and sit down quickly and write fifty.*

Then said he to another, *How much do you owe?* The debtor answered, *A hundred cors of wheat.* He said to him, *Take your bill and write eighty.*

The master commended the dishonest manager because he had done wisely – the children of this world are, in their own generation, wiser than the children of the light.

I tell you, make friends by means of unrighteous wealth so that, when you fail, they may receive you into the eternal tents.

Whoever is faithful in a very little is faithful also in much. Whoever is dishonest in a very little is dishonest also in much.

If therefore you have not been faithful with the unrighteous wealth, who will commit the true riches to your trust? If you have not been faithful in that which is another's, who will give you that which is your own?

༄ৡৢৣ৺

The Pharisees – who were lovers of money – heard all these things, and they scoffed at him.

He said to them,

You are those who justify yourselves in the sight of others, but God knows your hearts, and that which is exalted by people is an abomination in the sight of God.

The law and the prophets were there until John. From that time the good news of the kingdom of God is proclaimed, and everyone is forcing a way into it. But it is easier for heaven and earth to pass away than for one tiny stroke of a pen in the law to fall.

༄ৡৢৣ৺

There was a certain rich man, and he was clothed in purple and fine linen, living in luxury every day. At his gate lay a certain beggar, named Lazarus, full of sores and desiring to be fed with the crumbs that fell from the rich man's table. Yes, even the dogs came and licked his sores.

The beggar died and was carried away by the angels to Abraham's bosom.

The rich man also died and was buried. In hell, he lifted up his eyes in torment and saw Abraham far off, with Lazarus at his bosom. He cried out, *Father Abraham, have mercy on me, and send*

Lazarus, that he may dip the tip of his finger in water and cool my tongue, for I am in anguish in this flame.

But Abraham said, *Son, remember that you, in your lifetime, received your good things and Lazarus, in like manner, bad things. But now here he is comforted, and you are in anguish. Besides all this, there is a great gulf between you and us, so that those who want to pass from here to you are not able – and none may cross over from there to here.*

The rich man said, *I ask you, father, that you send him to my father's house – for I have five brothers – so that he may testify to them, and they will not also come into this place of torment.*

But Abraham said, *They have Moses and the prophets. Let them listen to them.*

He said, *No, father Abraham – if one but goes to them from the dead, they will repent.*

Abraham said to him, *If they do not listen to Moses and the prophets, neither will they be persuaded if one rises from the dead.*

Part 7

TESTAMENT
TO JOHN

TESTAMENT TO JOHN

An account of events related to
the testament to John by Jesus the Messiah

Part 7

John the baptizer is imprisoned

HEROD, THE TETRARCH, SENT out and arrested John, bound him, and shut him up in prison for the sake of Herodias, the wife of his brother Philip. Herod had married her, and John reproved him, saying, "It is not lawful for you to have your brother's wife."

Jesus extols John as prophet

While John was in the prison, Jesus cured many diseases and plagues and evil spirits, and he gave sight to many who were blind.

It happened that John called two of his disciples and sent them to Jesus to ask, "Are you the one who is coming, or should we look for another?" So the men went to Jesus and said, "John the baptizer has sent us to you to ask, 'Are you he who comes, or should we look for another?'"

Jesus answered them, "Go and tell John the things that you have seen and heard – the blind receive their sight, the lame walk, the lepers are cleansed, the deaf hear, the dead are raised up, and the poor have good news proclaimed to them. And blessed is he who is not offended by me."

As the messengers went their way to tell John about all the works of the Messiah, Jesus began to talk to the crowds about John,

What did you go out into the wilderness to see? A reed shaken by the wind?

What did you go out to see? A man clothed in soft clothing? Behold, those who wear soft clothing and live delicately are in kings' houses.

What did you go out to see? A prophet? Yes, I tell you, and much more than a prophet.

This is one about whom it is written, *Behold, I send my messenger ahead of you, who will prepare your way before you.*

Truly I tell you, among those born of women, there is not a greater prophet than John the baptizer. Yet he who is least in the kingdom of God is greater than he.

To what then will I liken the people of this generation? What are they like?

They are like children who sit in the marketplace, calling one to another, saying, *We played the flute for you, and you did not dance. We mourned for you, and you did not weep.*

John the baptizer came neither eating bread nor drinking wine, and they say, *He has a demon.* The Son of Man has come eating and drinking, and they say, *Behold, a gluttonous man and a drunkard, a friend of tax collectors and sinners.*

But wisdom is justified by all her children.

From the days of John the baptizer until now, the kingdom of heaven suffers violence, and the violent take by force – for all the prophets and the law prophesied until John, if you are willing to receive it, that Elijah is the one who is to come.

Let anyone hear who has ears to hear.

When all the people who had been baptized with John's baptism heard this, including the tax collectors, they declared God to be just.

But the Pharisees and the lawyers, who had not been baptized by him, rejected the counsel of God.

Herod orders the beheading of John

Herodias set herself against John and desired to have him put to death. But she could not, for Herod feared John, knowing that he was a righteous and holy man, and kept him safe. John did many things, and Herod heard him gladly. Herod also feared the crowd, because they counted him as a prophet.

Then a convenient day came when Herod on his birthday made a supper for his nobles, the high officers, and the chief leaders of Galilee.

The daughter of Herodias herself came in and danced among them and pleased Herod and those sitting with him. The king promised with an oath to her, "Whatever you shall ask of me, I will give you, up to half of my kingdom."

She went out and said to her mother, "What shall I ask?" And her mother replied, "The head of John the baptizer."

She came in immediately with haste to the king and, prompted by her mother, said, "I want you to give me right now the head of John the baptizer, here on a platter."

❦

The king was exceedingly grieved but, for the sake of his oaths and of those who sat at the table with him, he did not wish to refuse her and commanded it to be given.

Immediately, the king sent out a soldier of his guard and commanded him to bring John's head. The guard went and beheaded John in the prison, brought his head on a platter, and gave it to the young lady. She brought it to her mother.

When John's disciples heard this, they came and took up his corpse and laid it in a tomb. Then they went and told Jesus.

When Jesus heard, he withdrew in a boat to a deserted place apart, and the crowds followed him on foot from the cities.

Herod hears reports about Jesus

At that time, Herod heard the report about Jesus and all that was done by him — his name had become known.

Now Herod was very perplexed, because some said, "John the baptizer has risen from the dead, and powers are at work in him." Others said, "He is Elijah." Others said, "He is a prophet, like one of the prophets of old."

Herod said, "John I beheaded, but who is the one about whom I hear such things?" He sought to see him.

Part 8

JERUSALEM
SOJOURNS

JERUSALEM SOJOURNS

An account of events related to
sojourns to Jerusalem by Jesus the Messiah

Part 8

Jesus reveals the Father

AFTER THESE THINGS, THERE was a feast of the Jews, and Jesus went to Jerusalem.

Now in Jerusalem there is a pool by the sheep gate called Bethesda in Hebrew. It has five porches, and on these lay a great multitude of those who were sick, blind, lame, or paralyzed.

They waited for the moving of the water, for an angel of the Lord has come down at certain times into the pool and stirred up the water. Whoever stepped in first after the stirring of the water was made whole from whatever disease was had. A certain man was there, who had been sick for thirty-eight years.

When Jesus saw the man lying there, he knew that he had been sick for a long time and asked him, "Do you want to be made well?"

The sick man answered, "Sir, I have no one to put me into the pool when the water is stirred up – while I am coming, another steps down before me."

Jesus said to him, "Arise, take up your mat, and walk." Immediately, the man was made well, and he took up his mat and walked.

※❦※

Now it was the sabbath on that day. So the Jews said to the one who was cured, "It is the sabbath. It is not lawful for you to carry the mat."

He answered them, "He who made me well said to me, 'Take up your mat and walk.'"

They asked him, "Who is the man who said to you, 'Take up your mat and walk'?"

But the man who was healed did not know who it was, for Jesus had withdrawn from the crowd in that place. Afterward Jesus found him in the temple and said to him, "Behold, you are made well. Sin no more, so that nothing worse happens to you."

The man went away and told the Jews that it was Jesus who had made him well. And the Jews persecuted Jesus and sought to kill him, because he did these things on the sabbath.

But Jesus answered them, "My Father is still working, so I am working, too." For this cause the Jews sought all the more to kill him, because he not only broke the sabbath, but also called God his own Father, making himself equal with God.

Jesus answered,

> Truly I tell you, the Son can do nothing of himself, but what he sees the Father doing – whatever things he does, the Son does these likewise.

> For the Father has affection for the Son and shows him all things that he himself does. He will show him greater works than these, that you may marvel. As the Father raises the dead and gives them life, even so the Son gives life to whom he desires.

> The Father judges no one, but he has given all judgment to the Son, that all may honor the Son, even as they honor the Father. Anyone who does not honor the Son does not honor the Father who sent him.

Truly I tell you, anyone who hears my word and believes him who sent me has eternal life and does not come into judgment, but has passed out of death into life.

Truly I tell you, the hour comes, and is now here, when the dead will hear the voice of the Son of God, and those who hear will live.

As the Father has life in himself, even so he gave to the Son also to have life in himself, and he gave him authority to execute judgment, because he is the Son of Man.

Do not marvel at this, for the hour comes in which all that are in the tombs will hear his voice and will come out – those who have done good to the resurrection of life and those who have done evil to the resurrection of judgment.

I can of myself do nothing. As I hear, I judge, and my judgment is righteous, because I do not seek my own will, but the will of the one who sent me.

If I testify about myself, my witness is not valid. It is another who testifies about me, and I know that his testimony about me is true.

You sent messengers to John, and he testified to the truth. But the testimony that I receive is not from man. However, I say these things that you may be saved. He was the burning and shining lamp, and you were willing to rejoice for a while in his light. But the testimony that I have is greater than that of John.

The works that the Father gave me to accomplish, the very works that I do, testify that the Father has sent me.

The Father himself, who sent me, has testified about me. You have neither heard his voice nor seen his form. You do not have his word living in you, because you do not believe him whom he sent.

You search the scriptures because you think that in them you have eternal life, and they testify about me. Yet you will not come to me, so that you may have life.

I do not receive glory from people. But I know that you do not have God's love in yourselves – I have come in my Father's name, and you do not receive me. If another comes in his own name, you will receive him.

How can you believe when you receive glory from one another and do not seek the glory that comes from the only God?

Do not think that I will accuse you to the Father. There is one who accuses you – Moses – on whom you have set your hope. But, if you believed Moses, you would believe me, for he wrote about me. And if you do not believe his writings, how will you believe my words?

Jesus speaks openly

After these things, Jesus returned to Galilee and walked about there, for he would not walk in Judea because the Jews sought to kill him.

❦

When the feast of the Jews – the Feast of Booths – was at hand, his brothers said to him, "Depart from here and go into Judea, so that your disciples also may see the works that you do, for no one does anything in secret who seeks to be known openly. If you do these things, you will reveal yourself to the world," for his brothers did not believe in him.

Jesus said to them, "My time has not yet come, but your time is always ready. The world cannot hate you, but it hates me, because I testify about it, that its works are evil. You go to the feast. I am not going to this feast because my time is not yet fulfilled."

Having said these things to them, he stayed in Galilee.

❧❧❧

But after his brothers had gone to the feast, then he also went, not publicly but in secret.

The Jews sought him at the feast and said, "Where is he?" There was much murmuring about him among the crowds. Some said, "He is a good man." Others said, "Not so – he leads the multitude astray." Yet no one spoke openly of him for fear of the Jews.

❧❧❧

In the midst of the feast, Jesus went up into the temple and taught. The Jews marveled, saying, "How does this man know letters, having never been educated?"

Jesus answered them,

My teaching is not mine, but his who sent me. Anyone who desires to do his will knows about the teaching, whether it is from God or whether I am speaking from myself. Those who speak from themselves seek their own glory, but the one who seeks the glory of him who sent him is true, and no unrighteousness is in him.

Did Moses not give you the law, and yet none of you keeps the law?

Then he asked, "Why do you seek to kill me?"

The crowd answered, "You have a demon – who seeks to kill you?"

Jesus answered them,

I did one work, and you all marvel because of it. Moses has given you circumcision, and you circumcise a boy on the sabbath. If a

boy receives circumcision on the sabbath so that the law of Moses may not be broken, are you angry with me because I made a man completely healthy on the sabbath? Do not judge according to appearance, but with righteous judgment.

❧⚜❧

Some of them of Jerusalem said, "Is this not the one whom they seek to kill? Behold, he speaks openly, and they say nothing to him. Can it be that the rulers indeed know that this is truly the Messiah? However, we know where this man comes from but, when the Messiah comes, no one will know where he is from."

Just then Jesus cried out as he was teaching in the temple,

You both know me and know where I am from. I have not come of myself. But he who sent me is true, and you do not know him. I know him, because I am from him, and he sent me.

But many in the crowd believed in him. They said, "When the Messiah comes, will he do more signs than those which this man has done?"

The Pharisees heard the crowd murmuring these things about him, and the chief priests and the Pharisees sent officers to arrest him. They sought therefore to take him, but no one laid a hand on him, because his hour had not yet come.

Then Jesus said, "I will be with you a little while longer, then I will go to him who sent me. You will seek me and will not find me, and where I am you cannot come."

The Jews said among themselves, "Where will this man go that we will not find him? Will he go to the Dispersion among the Greeks and teach the Greeks? What is this word that he said, 'You will seek me and will not find me, and where I am you cannot come'?"

⁕🜍⁕

On the last and greatest day of the feast, Jesus stood and cried out,

Let anyone who is thirsty come to me and let the one who believes in me drink. The scripture has said, *From within him will flow rivers of living water.*

⁕🜍⁕

When they heard these words, many said, "This is truly the prophet." Others said, "This is the Messiah." But some said, "What? Does the Messiah come out of Galilee? Has the scripture not said that the Messiah comes from the seed of David and from Bethlehem – the village where David was?"

So there arose a division in the crowd because of him, and some of them would have arrested him. But no one laid hands on him.

⁕🜍⁕

The officers came back to the chief priests and Pharisees, who asked them, "Why did you not bring him?"

The officers answered, "No man ever spoke like this."

The Pharisees answered them, "You are not also led astray, are you? Have any of the rulers believed in him or any of the Pharisees? This crowd – that does not know the law – is accursed."

Nicodemus – one of them who came to Jesus by night – said to them, "Does our law judge a man unless it first hears from him personally and knows what he does?"

They answered him, "Are you also from Galilee? Search and see that no prophet has arisen out of Galilee."

Jesus provides testimony

All the people went to their own homes, but Jesus went to the Mount of Olives.

Very early in the morning, he came again into the temple. All the people came to him, and he sat down and taught them.

⁂

While he was teaching, the scribes and the Pharisees brought a woman taken in adultery. Having set her in the midst, they told him, "Teacher, we found this woman in adultery, in the very act. Now in our law, Moses commanded us to stone such. What then do you say about her?" They said this to test him, so that they might have something with which to accuse him.

Jesus stooped down and wrote on the ground with his finger. When they asked him, he looked up and said, "Let anyone among you who is without sin throw the first stone at her." Again he stooped down, and with his finger wrote on the ground.

When they heard it – being convicted by their conscience – they went out one by one, beginning from the oldest, and Jesus was left alone with the woman in the middle where she was.

Standing up, Jesus saw her and said, "Woman, where are your accusers? Did no one condemn you?"

She said, "No one, Lord." And Jesus said, "Neither do I condemn you. Go your way and, from now on, sin no more."

❦

Later, in the temple, Jesus again spoke to them, saying,

I am the light of the world. Those who follow me will not walk in the darkness but will have the light of life.

The Pharisees said to him, "You testify about yourself. Your testimony is not valid."

Jesus answered them,

Even if I testify about myself, my testimony is true, for I know where I came from and where I am going, but you do not know where I came from or where I am going.

You judge according to the flesh. I judge no one. Even if I do judge, my judgment is true, for I am not alone but am with the Father who sent me. It is written in your law that the testimony of two people is valid. I am one who testifies about myself, and the Father who sent me also testifies about me.

Then they asked, "Where is your Father?"

Jesus answered, "You know neither me nor my Father. If you knew me, you would know my Father also."

Jesus spoke these words in the treasury, as he taught in the temple. Yet no one arrested him, because his hour had not yet come.

Jesus then said again to them, "I am going away and you will seek me, and you will die in your sins. Where I go, you cannot come."

The Jews spoke among themselves, "Will he kill himself? Is that what he means when he says, 'Where I am going, you cannot come'?"

Jesus said to them, "You are from beneath. I am from above. You are of this world. I am not of this world. I said that you will die in your sins, for you will die in your sins unless you believe that I am he."

They said to him, "Who are you?"

And he said, "Just what have I been saying to you from the beginning? I have many things to speak and to judge concerning you. However, he who sent me is true, and the things which I heard from him – these I say to the world."

They did not understand that he spoke to them about the Father. So Jesus said,

> When you have lifted up the Son of Man, then you will know that I am he and that I do nothing of myself, but I say these things as my Father taught me.

> He who sent me is with me – the Father has not left me alone, for I always do the things that are pleasing to him.

As he spoke these things, many believed in him.

Jesus addresses descendency

Jesus said to those Jews who had believed him, "If you remain in my word, then you are truly my disciples. You will know the truth, and the truth will make you free."

They answered him, "We are of Abraham's seed and have never been in bondage to anyone. What do you mean when you say, 'You will be made free'?"

Jesus answered them,

Truly I tell you, everyone who commits sin is the bondservant of sin. A bondservant does not live in the house forever, but a son remains forever. If therefore the Son makes you free, you will be free indeed.

I know that you are of Abraham's seed, yet you seek to kill me, because my word finds no place in you. I speak about the things that I have seen with my Father, just as you also do the things that you have seen with your father.

They said, "Our father is Abraham."

Jesus declared,

If you were Abraham's children, you would do the works of Abraham. But now you seek to kill me – a man who has told you the truth, which I heard from God. Abraham did not do this. You indeed do the works of your father.

They said to him, "We were not born of sexual immorality. We have one father – God."

Jesus said to them,

If God were your father, you would love me, for I came out and have come from God. I have not come of myself, but he sent me.

Why do you not understand my speech? Because you cannot hear my word? You are of your father, the devil, and you want to do the desires of your father.

He was a murderer from the beginning and does not stand in the truth, because there is no truth in him. When he speaks a lie, he speaks on his own, for he is a liar – the father of lies. But because I tell the truth, you do not believe me.

Which of you convicts me of sin? If I tell the truth, why do you not believe me? Whoever is of God hears the word of God. For this cause you do not hear, because you are not of God.

The Jews answered him, "Do we not say well that you are a Samaritan and have a demon?"

Jesus answered,

I do not have a demon, but I honor my Father and you dishonor me. But I do not seek my own glory. There is one who seeks and judges. Truly I tell you, whoever keeps my word will never see death.

Then the Jews said to him, "Now we know that you have a demon. Abraham died, as did the prophets, and you say, 'If a man keeps my word, he will never taste of death.' Are you greater than our father, Abraham, who died? The prophets died. Who do you make yourself out to be?"

Jesus answered,

If I glorify myself, my glory is nothing. It is my Father who glorifies me – he of whom you say, *He is our God* – though you have not known him. But I know him.

If I said, *I do not know him,* I would be like you, a liar. But I know him and keep his word. Your father Abraham rejoiced to see my day – he saw it and was glad.

The Jews then said to him, "You are not yet fifty years old and you have seen Abraham?"

Jesus said to them, "Truly I tell you, before Abraham came into existence, I am."

They took up stones to throw at him, but Jesus hid and went out of the temple.

Jesus opens eyes of the blind

As he passed along, he saw a man blind from birth.

His disciples asked him, "Rabbi, who sinned – this man or his parents – that he was born blind?"

Jesus answered,

Neither did this man sin, nor his parents, but he was born blind so that the works of God might be revealed in him. I must work the works of him who sent me while it is day – the night is coming, when no one can work.

While I am in the world, I am the light of the world.

When he had said this, he spat on the ground, made mud with the saliva, anointed the blind man's eyes with the mud, and said to him, "Go, wash in the pool of Siloam."

So the man went away, washed, and came back seeing.

❦

The neighbors and those who saw that he was blind before said, "Is this not he who sat and begged?" Some said, "It is he." Others were saying, "It looks like him."

But the man said, "I am he."

So they asked him, "How were your eyes opened?"

He answered, "A man called Jesus made mud, anointed my eyes, and said to me, 'Go to the pool of Siloam and wash.' So I went away and washed, and I received sight."

Then they asked him, "Where is he?"

He said, "I do not know."

⁓ᴥ⬥ᴥ⁓

They brought the man who had been blind to the Pharisees. The Pharisees also asked him how he received his sight. The man said to them, "He put mud on my eyes, I washed, and I see."

It was a sabbath when Jesus made the mud and opened his eyes, and some of the Pharisees said, "This man is not from God, because he does not keep the sabbath."

But others said, "How can a man who is a sinner do such signs?" There was division among them. They asked the blind man again, "What do you say about him since he opened your eyes?"

The man said, "He is a prophet."

⁓ᴥ⬥ᴥ⁓

The Jews did not believe that he had been blind and had received his sight until they called the parents of the man and asked them, "Is this your son, who you say was born blind? How then does he now see?"

His parents answered them, "We know that this is our son and that he was born blind, but we do not know how he now sees, and we do not know who opened his eyes. Ask him – he is of age. He will speak for himself."

His parents said these things because they feared the Jews, for the Jews had already agreed that anyone who confessed him as the Messiah would be put out of the synagogue.

❦

So they called the man who had been blind a second time and said to him, "Give glory to God. We know that this man is a sinner."

He answered, "I do not know if he is a sinner. One thing I do know – though I was blind, now I see."

They asked him again, "What did he do to you? How did he open your eyes?"

He answered them, "I told you already, and you did not listen. Why do you want to hear it again? Do you also want to become his disciples?"

They insulted him and said, "You are his disciple, but we are disciples of Moses. We know that God has spoken to Moses. But, as for this man, we do not know where he comes from."

The man answered, "How amazing. You do not know where he comes from, yet he opened my eyes. We know that God does not listen to sinners, but he listens to anyone who is a worshipper of God and does his will. Never since the world began has it been heard that anyone opened the eyes of someone born blind. If this man were not from God, he could do nothing."

They answered him, "You were altogether born in sin, and now you teach us?" They threw him out.

Jesus heard that they had thrown him out and, finding him, he said, "Do you believe in the Son of God?"

He answered, "Who is he, Lord? Tell me so that I may believe in him."

Jesus said to him, "You have seen him, and it is he who speaks with you."

He said, "Lord, I believe." And he worshiped him.

Jesus said, "I came into this world for judgment, so that those who do not see may see and those who see may become blind."

Those of the Pharisees who were with him heard these things and said to him, "Are we also blind?"

Jesus said to them,

If you were blind, you would have no sin, but now that you say, *We see,* your sin remains.

Truly I tell you, one who does not enter by the door into the sheepfold but climbs up some other way is a thief and a robber.

The one who enters in by the door is the shepherd of the sheep. The gatekeeper opens the gate for him, and the sheep listen to his voice. He calls his own sheep by name and leads them out.

When he brings out his own sheep, he goes before them, and the sheep follow him for they know his voice. They will by no means follow a stranger but will flee from him, for they do not know the voice of strangers.

Jesus spoke this parable to them, but they did not understand what he was telling them. Therefore Jesus said to them,

Truly I tell you, I am the sheep's door. All who came before me are thieves and robbers, but the sheep did not listen to them.

I am the door. Anyone who enters in by me will be saved and will go in and go out and will find pasture. The thief only comes to steal, kill, and destroy.

I came that they may have life and have it abundantly. I am the good shepherd. The good shepherd lays down his life for the sheep.

He who is a hired hand and not a shepherd, who does not own the sheep, sees the wolf coming, leaves the sheep, and flees. The wolf snatches the sheep and scatters them. The hired hand flees because he is a hired hand and does not care for the sheep.

I am the good shepherd. I know my own, and I am known by my own, even as the Father knows me and I know the Father. I have other sheep, which are not of this fold. I must bring them also, and they will hear my voice. They will become one flock with one shepherd.

I lay down my life for the sheep. The Father loves me because I lay down my life that I may take it up again. No one takes it away from me, but I lay it down by myself. I have power to lay it down, and I have power to take it up again.

I received this commandment from my Father.

A division arose again among the Jews because of these words. Many of them said, "He has a demon and is insane. Why do you listen to him?"

Others said, "These are not the sayings of one possessed by a demon. It is not possible for a demon to open the eyes of the blind, is it?"

Jesus escapes arrest

It was winter when the Feast of the Dedication took place in Jerusalem. At that time, Jesus was walking in the temple, on Solomon's porch.

The Jews came around him and said to him, "How long will you hold us in suspense? If you are the Messiah, tell us plainly."

Jesus answered them,

I told you, and you do not believe. The works that I do in my Father's name testify about me. But you do not believe because you are not of my sheep.

My sheep hear my voice and I know them and they follow me. I give eternal life to them. They will never perish, and no one will snatch them out of my hand.

My Father, who has given them to me, is greater than all. No one is able to snatch them out of my Father's hand. The Father and I are one.

The Jews took up stones again to stone him.

Jesus answered them, "I have shown you many good works from my Father. For which of those works do you stone me?"

The Jews answered, "We do not stone you for a good work, but for blasphemy, because you – being a man – make yourself God."

Jesus answered them,

Is it not written in your law, *I said, 'You are gods'?*

If those to whom the word of God came were called *gods* – and the scripture cannot be broken – do you say of the one whom the Father sanctified and sent into the world, *You blaspheme,* because I said, *I am the Son of God?*

If I do not do the works of my Father, do not believe me. But, if I do them, though you do not believe me, believe the works, so that you may know and believe that the Father is in me and I am in the Father.

They sought again to seize him, and he escaped from their hands.

Part 9

ILLUMINATIONS

ILLUMINATIONS

An account of events related to
certain illuminations of Jesus the Messiah

Part 9

Jesus sustains the crowd

AFTER JESUS RETURNED, HE went away to Bethsaida on the other side of the Sea of Galilee. A great crowd followed him because they saw the signs that he did on those who were sick.

Jesus went up on the mountain, and he sat there with his disciples.

Now the Passover, the feast of the Jews, was at hand. When he lifted his eyes, he saw a great crowd coming to him, and he had compassion on them, because they were harassed and scattered, like sheep without a shepherd. He began to teach them many things.

꙳ᕯ꙳

When the day began to wear away and evening had come, Jesus said to the twelve, "Where are we to buy bread, so that these people may eat?"

Philip answered him, "Two hundred denarii worth of bread would not be sufficient for every one of them to receive even a little."

The other disciples said, "This place is deserted, and the hour is already late. Send the crowd away – they may go into the surrounding villages and farms and buy themselves food."

But Jesus said to them, "They do not need to go away. You give them something to eat."

They asked him, "Shall we go and buy two hundred denarii worth of bread and give it to them?"

He said, "How many loaves do you have? Go see."

When they knew, one of his disciples, Andrew, reported to him, "There is a boy here who has five barley loaves and two fish. But what are these among so many?"

Jesus said, "Bring them here to me."

He said to his disciples, "Make them sit down in groups of about fifty each."

They did so and made them all sit down in groups on the green grass, about five thousand altogether.

He took the five loaves and the two fish and, looking up to heaven, he blessed and broke the loaves, and he gave to his disciples to set before them. And he divided the two fish among them all.

They all ate and were filled.

When they were done, Jesus said to his disciples, "Gather up the broken pieces that are left over, so that nothing is lost."

So they gathered them up and filled twelve baskets with broken pieces from the five barley loaves – left over by those who had eaten.

When the people saw the sign that Jesus did, they said, "This is truly the prophet who comes into the world."

꙳ꙮ꙳

Jesus perceived that they were about to come and take him by force to make him king, and he immediately made his disciples go down to the sea while he himself sent the crowd away.

His disciples got into the boat to go ahead to the other side. After Jesus had taken leave of them, they started to go over the sea to Capernaum, and he went up again to the mountain by himself to pray.

❧✦☙

When evening came, he was alone on the land, and the boat was in the midst of the sea – the disciples had rowed about twenty-five or thirty stadia.

It was now dark, and the boat was distressed by the waves, for a great wind was blowing.

In the fourth watch of the night, Jesus walked toward them on the sea.

He would have passed by them but, seeing them rowing in distress in the contrary wind, he came to them.

The disciples saw him walking on the sea, drawing near to the boat, and they were afraid. They supposed that it was a ghost, and cried out in fear.

Immediately, Jesus spoke to them, saying, "Take heart – it is I. Do not be afraid."

Simon answered him, "Lord, if it is you, command me to come to you on the waters."

Jesus said, "Come."

Simon stepped down from the boat and walked on the waters toward Jesus. But when he felt the strong wind, he was afraid and, beginning to sink, he cried out, "Lord, save me."

Jesus stretched out his hand, took hold of him, and said, "You of little faith, why did you doubt?"

They got into the boat, and the wind ceased. The disciples were amazed and marveled among themselves, for their hearts were hardened and they had not understood about the loaves. Then they worshiped him, saying, "You are truly the Son of God."

⁕ᴥ⁕

Soon the boat came to land at Gennesaret, and they moored it to the shore. When they got out, people of that place recognized Jesus immediately and ran to send word into all that surrounding region, and they began to bring the sick on their mats to him.

Jesus speaks of bread from heaven

The next day, the crowd that stood on the other side of the sea saw that Jesus was not there, nor his disciples.

They also saw that his disciples had gone away alone – that Jesus had not entered into the boat with them – and that there had been no other boat except the one in which the disciples embarked.

However, other boats came near to the place where they ate the bread. The crowd therefore got into the boats and came to Capernaum, seeking Jesus.

⁕ᴥ⁕

When they found him on the other side of the sea, they asked him, "Rabbi, when did you come here?"

Jesus answered them, "Truly I tell you, you seek me not because you saw signs, but because you ate of the loaves and were filled. Do not work for the food which perishes but for the food which remains to eternal life, which the Son of Man will give to you – for God the Father has sealed him."

They said, "What must we do in order to work the works of God?"

Jesus answered, "This is the work of God – that you believe in him whom he has sent."

They said to him, "What then do you do for a sign, so that we may see and believe you? What work do you do? Our forebears ate the manna in the wilderness, as it is written, 'He gave them bread out of heaven to eat.'"

Jesus said to them, "Truly I tell you, it was not Moses who gave you the bread out of heaven. It is my Father who gives you the true bread out of heaven, for the bread of God is that which comes down out of heaven and gives life to the world."

They said to him, "Lord, give us this bread always."

Jesus said to them,

I am the bread of life. Whoever comes to me will not be hungry, and whoever believes in me will never be thirsty.

All that the Father gives will come to me, and I will in no way throw out anyone who comes to me, for I have come down from heaven, not to do my own will, but to do the will of him who sent me.

This is the will of the one who sent me – that I should lose nothing of all he has given to me but should raise him up on the last day. This is the will of my Father – that everyone who sees the Son and believes in him should have eternal life, and I will raise him up on the last day.

But you have seen me, and you do not yet believe.

※🜚🜚🜛※

The Jews murmured about him because he said, "I am the bread that came down out of heaven." They said, "Is this not Jesus, the son of Joseph, whose father and mother we know? How then does he say, 'I have come down out of heaven'?"

Jesus answered them,

Do not murmur among yourselves. No one can come to me unless drawn by the Father who sent me, and I will raise that one up in the last day. It is written in the prophets, *They will all be taught by God.*

Everyone who has heard and learned from the Father comes to me. Not that anyone has seen the Father except the one who is from God – he has seen the Father.

Truly I tell you, whoever believes in me has eternal life.

I am the bread of life. Your forebears ate the manna in the wilderness, and they died. This is the bread that comes down out of heaven, so that anyone may eat of it and not die.

I am the living bread that came down out of heaven. Anyone who eats of this bread will live forever, and the bread that I will give for the life of the world is my flesh.

The Jews then contended with one another, saying, "How can this man give us his flesh to eat?"

Jesus said to them,

Truly I tell you, unless you eat the flesh of the Son of Man and drink his blood, you do not have life in yourselves.

Those who eat my flesh and drink my blood have eternal life, and I will raise them up on the last day, for my flesh is food indeed and my blood is drink indeed.

Those who eat my flesh and drink my blood live in me, and I in them. As the living Father sent me – I live because of the Father, so whoever feeds on me will also live because of me.

This is the bread that came down out of heaven, not as your forebears ate. The one who eats this bread will live forever.

He said these things as he taught in the synagogue in Capernaum.

❦

When many of his disciples heard this, they said, "This is a hard saying – who can listen to it?"

But Jesus, knowing that his disciples murmured at this, said to them,

Does this cause you to stumble? Then what if you would see the Son of Man ascending to where he was before?

It is the Spirit who gives life – the flesh profits nothing – and the words that I speak to you are spirit and life.

But there are some of you who do not believe. For this cause I have said to you that no one can come to me unless it is given by my Father.

❦

At this, many of his disciples went back and walked no more with him.

Jesus said to the twelve, "Do you also want to go away?"

Simon answered him, "Lord, to whom would we go? You have the words of eternal life. We have come to believe and know that you are the Messiah, the Son of the living God."

Jesus replied, "Did I not choose you, the twelve? Yet one of you is a devil."

Jesus distinguishes defilement

When the Pharisees and some of the scribes from Jerusalem came to Jesus and gathered together, they saw some of his disciples eating bread with defiled – that is, unwashed – hands, and they found fault.

They asked him, "Why do your disciples disobey the tradition of the elders and eat their bread with unwashed hands?"

He answered them,

Why do you also disobey the commandment of God because of your tradition? For God commanded, *Honor your father and your mother,* and, *Whoever speaks evil of father or mother must be put to death.* But you say that whoever may tell father or mother, *Whatever help you might otherwise have gotten from me is a gift devoted to God,* shall not honor his father or mother. Then you no longer allow that one to do anything for the father or mother.

You have made the commandment of God void by your tradition. And you do many other such things – full well do you reject the commandment of God, so that you may keep your tradition.

Then he said to them,

Well did Isaiah prophesy of you hypocrites, as it is written, *This people honors me with their lips, but their hearts are far from me – in vain do they worship me, teaching human commandments as doctrines.*

He summoned the crowd and said,

Hear me, all of you, and understand – that which enters into the mouth does not defile the person. It is that which proceeds out of the mouth that defiles.

Let anyone hear who has ears to hear.

※※

When he entered into a house away from the crowd, the disciples came and said, "Do you know that the Pharisees were offended when they heard this saying?"

He answered, "Every plant that my heavenly Father did not plant will be uprooted. Leave them alone – they are blind guides of the blind and, if the blind guide the blind, both will fall into a pit."

Then his disciples asked him about the parable. Simon said, "Explain the parable to us."

Jesus said,

Do you also still not understand? Do you not understand that whatever goes into the mouth and passes into the belly cannot defile because it does not go into the heart, but into the stomach, then into the latrine? But the things which proceed out of the mouth come out of the heart, and they defile.

Evil proceeds from within, out of the heart. Adulteries, sexual sins, murders, thefts, coveting, wickedness, deceit, false testimony, lustful desires, an evil eye, blasphemy, pride, foolishness – all these evil things come from within and defile the person.

Jesus ventures to Tyre and Sidon

Jesus went away from there and withdrew into the region of Tyre and Sidon. Wherever he entered – into villages, cities, or the country – they laid the sick in the marketplaces and begged him that they might touch just the fringe of his garment. All who touched it were made well.

⁂

In one place, he entered a house and did not want anyone to know it. But he could not escape notice – a Canaanite woman from those borders, whose little daughter had an unclean spirit, heard about him and came and begged him to cast the demon out of her daughter. She cried, "Have mercy on me, Lord, son of David. My daughter is severely demonized."

Now the woman was a Greek, a Syrophoenician by race, and Jesus answered her not a word. His disciples came and urged him, "Send her away, for she cries after us."

He answered, "I was not sent to anyone but the lost sheep of the house of Israel."

But she came and worshiped him and fell down at his feet, saying, "Lord, help me."

But Jesus said to her, "Let the children be filled first, for it is not appropriate to take the children's bread and throw it to the dogs."

She said, "Yes, Lord, but even the dogs eat the crumbs which fall from their masters' table."

Then he answered, "Woman, great is your faith. For this saying, go your way – let it be done to you even as you desire. The demon has gone out of your daughter."

She went away to her house and found the child lying on the bed, with the demon gone.

※ᴖ❁ᴖ※

Jesus went out with his disciples into the villages of Caesarea Philippi and on the way he asked them, "Who do people say that I am?"

They told him, "Some say John the baptizer, others say Elijah, still others say Jeremiah or another of the old prophets."

He asked, "But who do you say that I am?"

Simon answered, "You are the Messiah, the Son of the living God."

Jesus said to him,

Blessed are you, Simon Bar Jonah, for flesh and blood has not revealed this to you, but my Father who is in heaven.

I also tell you that you are Cephas, and on this rock I will build my assembly, and the gates of hell will not prevail against it.

I will give to you the keys of the kingdom of heaven, and whatever you bind on earth will be bound in heaven, and whatever you release on earth will be released in heaven.

Then he commanded the disciples not to tell anyone about him, and he began to teach them, saying,

> The Son of Man must go to Jerusalem and suffer many things and be rejected by the elders, the chief priests, and scribes, and be killed, and on the third day rise again.

He spoke to them openly.

But Simon took him aside and began to rebuke him, saying, "Far be it from you, Lord. This will never be done to you."

Turning around and seeing his disciples, Jesus rebuked Simon and said, "Get behind me, Satan. You are a stumbling block to me, for you are not setting your mind on the things of God, but on the human things."

Then he said to all,

> Anyone who desires to come after me must deny oneself, take up the cross, and follow me. For whoever desires to save one's life will lose it, and whoever loses one's life for my sake and the sake of the good news will find it.

> How does it profit to gain the whole world and lose or forfeit one's own self? And what can one give in exchange for life?

> There are those in this adulterous and sinful generation who are ashamed of me and of my words. Of them the Son of Man also will be ashamed when he comes with the holy angels in his glory and the glory of his Father. Then he will render to all according to their deeds.

> Truly I tell you, there are some standing here who will in no way taste death until they see the Son of Man coming with power in the kingdom of God.

⁂

Jesus departed from the borders of Tyre and Sidon and came to the Sea of Galilee, in the region of Decapolis.

He went up the mountain and sat there. Great crowds came to him – with the lame, maimed, blind, mute, and many others.

They put them at his feet, and he healed them. The crowd wondered when they saw the mute speaking, the injured whole, the lame walking, and the blind seeing.

※〜〜※

They brought one who was deaf to him who also had an impediment in his speech. They begged Jesus to lay his hand on him.

Jesus took him aside privately. He put his fingers into the man's ears, then he spat and touched the man's tongue. Looking up to heaven, he sighed and said, "Ephphatha" – that is, "Be opened." Immediately, the man's ears were opened, and the impediment of his tongue was released and he spoke clearly.

Jesus commanded them that they should tell no one, but the more he commanded them, the more widely they proclaimed it.

They were astonished beyond measure, saying, "He has done all things well – he makes even the deaf hear and the mute speak." And they glorified the God of Israel.

※〜〜※

In those days, there was again a great crowd with nothing to eat, and Jesus summoned his disciples and said, "I have compassion for the crowd, because they have stayed with me now three days and have nothing to eat. I do not want to send them away to their homes fasting, for they might faint on the way – some of them have come a long way."

His disciples answered him, "Where should we get so many loaves in a deserted place that could satisfy so great a multitude?"

Jesus asked them, "How many loaves do you have?" They said, "Seven, and a few small fish."

※꙰꙰꙰※

Jesus commanded the crowd to sit down on the ground, and he took the seven loaves. Having given thanks, he broke them and gave them to his disciples to serve, and they served the multitude.

Then he took the few small fish. Having blessed them, he told his disciples to serve these also.

There were about four thousand people, and all ate and were filled. And they took up of the broken pieces that were left over, seven baskets full.

After Jesus sent the crowds away, he immediately got into the boat, and with his disciples came into the region of Magdala.

※꙰꙰꙰※

The Pharisees and Sadducees came to Jesus and began to question him. To test him, they asked him for a sign from heaven.

He sighed deeply in his spirit and said,

You know how to discern the appearance of the sky. When it is evening, you say, *It will be fair weather, for the sky is red.* In the

morning, you say, *It will be foul weather today, for the sky is red and threatening.* But you cannot discern the signs of the times.

An evil and adulterous generation seeks after a sign but, truly I tell you, no sign will be given to this generation except the sign of the prophet Jonah.

Then he left them and departed. Again entering into the boat, he went across and departed to the other side.

⁂

The disciples had forgotten to take bread and, when they came to the other side, they did not have more than one loaf in the boat with them.

Jesus warned them, saying, "Take heed and beware of the yeast of the Pharisees and Sadducees."

They reasoned among themselves, saying, "It is because we brought no bread."

Perceiving it, Jesus said to them, "Why do you reason that it is because you have no bread? Do you not yet perceive nor understand? Is your heart still hardened? Having eyes, do you not see? Having ears, do you not hear? Do you not remember, when I broke the five loaves among the five thousand, how many baskets full of broken pieces you took up?"

They told him, "Twelve."

And he asked, "When the seven loaves fed the four thousand, how many baskets full of broken pieces did you take up?"

They told him, "Seven."

Then he said, "Do you not yet understand? How is it that you do not perceive that I did not speak to you about bread? Beware of the yeast of the Pharisees and Sadducees."

Then they understood that he did not tell them to beware of the yeast of bread, but of the teaching of the Pharisees and Sadducees.

⁂

He came to Bethsaida.

Some people brought a blind man to Jesus and begged him to touch him. He took hold of the blind man by the hand and brought him out of the village. When he had spit on his eyes, he laid his hands on him and asked him if he saw anything.

The man looked up, and said, "I see men, but they look like trees walking." Then Jesus again laid his hands on the man's eyes. He looked intently and sight was restored, and he saw everyone clearly.

Jesus sent him away to his house, saying, "Do not tell anyone. Do not even enter into the village."

Jesus is in glory on the mountain

Some days later, Jesus took Simon and the brothers James and John with him, and brought them up a high mountain, by themselves, to pray.

As he was praying, he was transfigured before them. The appearance of his face was altered – it shone like the sun – and his clothing became dazzling white.

They saw his glory and, behold, two men appeared to them – Moses and Elijah – who stood talking with Jesus. They spoke of his departure, which he was about to accomplish at Jerusalem.

Simon said to Jesus, "Rabbi, it is good for us to be here. Let us make three tents – one for you, one for Moses, and one for Elijah."

While he was speaking, a bright cloud came and overshadowed them, and they were afraid. Out of the cloud came a voice,

This is my Son, my beloved Son, in whom I am well pleased. Listen to him.

When the disciples heard it, they fell on their faces and were very afraid. Jesus came and touched them and said, "Get up and do not be afraid."

Suddenly lifting up their eyes, they saw no one with them any more, except Jesus alone.

⁂

As they were coming down from the mountain, Jesus commanded them to tell no one what things they had seen, until after the Son of Man had risen from the dead.

So they kept this to themselves, questioning what the reference to rising from the dead meant.

⁂

Later, his disciples asked him, "Why do the scribes say that Elijah must come first?"

Jesus answered,

Elijah indeed comes first to restore all things.

How then is it written about the Son of Man – that he should suffer many things and be despised?

But I tell you that Elijah has already come, but they did not recognize him and they have done to him whatever they wanted.

So also will the Son of Man suffer by them.

The disciples understood that he spoke to them of John the baptizer.

And they were silent – in those days they told no one any of the things that they had seen.

Part 10

ADMONITIONS

ADMONITIONS

An account of events related to
certain admonitions of Jesus the Messiah

Part 10

Jesus comes down from the mountain

ON THE NEXT DAY, they came down from the mountain, and they saw the disciples with scribes questioning them and a great crowd around them.

Behold, a man from the crowd came to Jesus.

Kneeling down to him, he said, "Lord, I beg you to have mercy on my son, my only child. He is epileptic and suffers grievously from a mute spirit. The spirit seizes him, and he suddenly cries out. It throws him down and convulses him so that he foams at the mouth and grinds his teeth and wastes away. I brought him to your disciples and begged them to cast it out, but they were not able."

When the crowd saw Jesus, all were immediately amazed and ran to greet him.

He asked the scribes, "What are you asking them?"

Then he said, "Faithless and perverse generation, how long shall I be with you? How long shall I bear with you?" Then to the man, he said, "Bring your son here to me."

They brought the boy to him.

※❀❀❀※

When the demon saw Jesus, the spirit immediately convulsed the boy, and he fell on the ground, wallowing and foaming at the mouth.

Jesus asked his father, "How long has it been since this has come to him?"

The father answered, "From childhood. Often it has cast him both into the fire and into the water, to destroy him. If you can do anything, have compassion on us and help us."

Jesus said to him, "If you can believe, all things are possible to one who believes."

Immediately, the father of the child cried out with tears, "I believe. Help my unbelief."

Jesus rebuked the unclean spirit, saying, "You mute and deaf spirit, I command you, come out of him and never enter him again."

Having cried out and convulsed the boy violently, the demon came out, and the boy became like one dead — so much so that most of them said, "He is dead."

But Jesus took him by the hand and raised him up, and the boy arose.

Jesus gave the boy back to his father, and they were all astonished at the majesty of God.

※⁓❦⁓※

The disciples came to Jesus privately and asked, "Why were we not able to cast it out?"

He said to them, "Because of your unbelief."

The apostles said to the Lord, "Increase our faith," and the Lord said,

> Truly I tell you, if you had faith like a grain of mustard seed, you could tell this mountain, *Move from here to there,* and it would move. If you had faith like a grain of mustard seed, you could tell this sycamore tree, *Be uprooted and be planted in the sea,* and it would obey you. Nothing would be impossible for you.

> Who among you, having a servant plowing or keeping sheep, would say, when he comes in from the field, *Come immediately and sit down at the table?*

> Would you not rather tell him, *Prepare my supper, clothe yourself properly, and serve me, while I eat and drink. Afterward you shall eat and drink?* And do you thank that servant because he did the things that were commanded?

> I think not. So you also say, when you have done all the things that are commanded you, *We are unworthy servants. We have done our duty.*

> This kind of belief can come out by nothing, except by prayer and fasting.

Jesus returns to Capernaum

They came to Capernaum. When they first arrived, those who collected the didrachma coins came to Simon and said, "Does your teacher not pay the didrachma?"

Simon said, "Yes."

When he came into the house, Jesus anticipated him, saying, "What do you think, Simon? From whom do the kings of the earth receive toll or tribute? From their children or from strangers?"

When Simon said, "From strangers," Jesus said to him, "Therefore the children are exempt. But, lest we cause them to stumble, go to the sea and cast a hook. Take the first fish that comes up and, when you open its mouth, you will find a stater coin. Take that and give it to them for you and me."

⁂

When he was in the house, he asked them, "What were you arguing among yourselves on the way?" But they were silent, for an argument arose among them on the way about which of them was the greatest.

Jesus, perceiving the reasoning of their hearts, sat down, called the twelve, and said to them,

Whoever wants to be first shall be last of all and servant of all.

Then he called a little child to himself and set it in the midst of them. Taking it in his arms, he said to them,

Truly I tell you, unless you turn and become as little children, you will in no way enter into the kingdom of heaven.

Whoever becomes humble as this little child is the greatest in the kingdom of heaven. Whoever receives one such little child in my name receives me, and whoever receives me receives him who sent me, for whoever is least among you all will be the great one.

Do not cause one of these little ones to stumble. Whoever causes one of these little ones who believe in me to stumble, it would be better for you to be thrown into the depths of the sea with a huge millstone hung around your neck.

Woe to the world because of occasions of stumbling. The occasions must come, but woe to that person through whom the occasion comes.

If your hand causes you to stumble, cut it off and cast it away. It is better for you to enter into life maimed than to have your two hands and go to hell, the unquenchable fire.

If your foot causes you to stumble, cut it off and cast it away. It is better for you to enter into life maimed or crippled than to have two feet and be cast into hell, into the eternal fire.

If your eye causes you to stumble, pluck it out and cast it away. It is better for you to enter into the kingdom of God with one eye than to have two eyes and be cast into the hell of fire, *where their worm does not die and the fire is not quenched.*

Everyone will be salted with fire. Salt is good but, if the salt loses its saltiness and becomes flat and tasteless, with what will you season it? It is fit neither for the soil nor for the manure pile – it is thrown out.

Have salt in yourselves, and be at peace with one another.

✦✦✦

Later, he spoke to the crowds,

When you see a cloud rising from the west, you immediately say, *A shower is coming,* and so it happens. When a south wind blows, you say, *There will be a scorching heat,* and it happens. You hypocrites, you know how to interpret the appearance of the earth and the sky, but how is it that you do not interpret this time?

At that time, there were some present who told him about the Galileans whose blood Pilate had mixed with their sacrifices.

Jesus asked them,

Do you think that these Galileans were worse sinners than all the other Galileans because they suffered such things? I tell you, no, but, unless you repent, you will all perish in the same way.

Or those eighteen killed when the tower in Siloam fell on them – do you think that they were worse offenders than all those who dwell in Jerusalem? I tell you, no, but, unless you repent, you will all perish in the same way.

Then he told this parable,

A certain man had a fig tree planted in his vineyard, and he came seeking fruit on it and found none.

He said to the vine dresser, *Behold, for three years I have come looking for fruit on this fig tree and found none. Cut it down. Why let it waste the soil?*

He answered, *Lord, leave it alone this year also, until I dig around it and fertilize it. If it bears fruit, fine, but if not, you can cut it down after that.*

Jesus speaks on sabbath days

Jesus was teaching in one of the synagogues on the sabbath day and, behold, there was a woman who had a spirit of infirmity for eighteen years. She was bent over and could in no way straighten herself up.

When Jesus saw her, he called her and said, "Woman, you are freed from your infirmity." He laid his hands on her, and immediately she stood up straight and glorified God.

The ruler of the synagogue, indignant because Jesus had healed on the sabbath, said to the crowd, "There are six days in which people ought to work. Come on those days and be healed, not on the sabbath day." Jesus answered him,

You hypocrites, does not each one of you free your ox or donkey from the stall on the sabbath and lead it away to water?

> So ought not this woman, being a daughter of Abraham bound
> by Satan for eighteen long years, be freed from this bondage on the
> sabbath day?

As he said these things, all his adversaries were disappointed, and all the crowd rejoiced for the glorious things that were done by him.

٭ﺾﻟ٭

When Jesus went into the house of one of the rulers of the Pharisees on a sabbath to eat bread, they were watching him.

Behold, in front of him, there was a certain man who had dropsy.

Jesus asked the lawyers and Pharisees, "Is it lawful to heal on the sabbath?" But they were silent. So Jesus took the man and healed him and let him go.

Then he asked them, "Which of you, if your ox or donkey fell into a well, would not immediately pull him out on a sabbath day?"

They could not answer him regarding these things.

٭ﺾﻟ٭

When he noticed how the invited guests chose the best seats, he told them a parable,

> When you are invited by anyone to a marriage feast, do not sit in
> the best seat, since perhaps someone more honorable than you
> might be invited, and he who invited both of you would come and
> tell you, *Make room for this person.* Then you would begin, with
> shame, to take the lowest place.

But when you are invited, go and sit in the lowest place, so that when he who invited you comes, he may tell you, *Friend, move up higher.* Then you will be honored in the presence of all who sit at the table with you.

All who exalt themselves will be humbled, and all who humble themselves will be exalted.

He also said to the one who had invited him,

When you make a dinner or a supper, do not call your friends or your brothers, your kinsmen or rich neighbors, or perhaps they might return the favor and pay you back.

Instead, when you make a feast, ask the poor and the maimed, the lame and the blind, and you will be blessed, because they do not have the resources to repay you.

You will be repaid in the resurrection of the righteous.

﹡〜⟨✵⟩〜﹡

Someone at the table who heard these things said to him, "Blessed is he who will feast in the kingdom of God."

And Jesus said,

The kingdom of heaven is like a certain king, who made a marriage feast for his son and invited many.

At supper time, he sent out his servant to tell those who were invited to the marriage feast, *Come, for everything is ready now,* but they all as one began to make excuses and would not come.

That servant came and told his lord these things.

The king sent out other servants, saying, *Tell those who are invited, 'Behold, I have made ready my dinner – my cattle and my fatlings are killed, and all things are ready. Come to the marriage feast.'*

But they made light of it.

One said, *I have bought a field, and I must go and see it. Please have me excused,* and went to his farm. Another said, *I have bought five yoke of oxen, and I must go try them out. Please have me excused.* He went away to his merchandise. Another said, *I have married a wife, and therefore I cannot come,* and went his way. The rest grabbed his servants, treated them shamefully, and then killed them.

When the king heard this, he was angry and sent his armies to destroy those murderers and burn their city.

Then he said to his servants, *The wedding is ready, but those who were invited were not worthy. Go out quickly into the streets and lanes of the city and invite to the marriage feast as many as you may find. Bring in the poor, the maimed, the blind, and the lame.*

The servants returned and said, *Lord, it is done as you commanded, and there is still room.*

The lord said to the servants, *Go out into the highways and hedges and compel people to come in, so that my house may be filled. I tell you that none of those who were invited will taste my supper.*

Those servants went out into the highways and gathered together as many as they found, both bad and good. The wedding was filled with guests.

But when the king came in to see the guests, he saw a man who did not have on wedding clothing, and he said to him, *Friend, how did you come in here not wearing wedding clothing?*

The man was speechless.

Then the king said to the servants, *Bind him hand and foot, take him away, and throw him into the outer darkness, where there will be weeping and grinding of teeth.*

Many are called, but few are chosen.

Jesus cautions his disciples

John said to him, "Teacher, we saw someone casting out demons in your name, and we forbade him because he does not follow with us."

But Jesus said,

Do not forbid him, for no one who does a mighty work in my name is able quickly to speak evil of me. Whoever is not against us is for us.

Truly I tell you, whoever gives you a cup of water to drink in my name, because you are of the Messiah, will in no way lose the reward.

⁂

Jesus said to his disciples,

Be careful. If your brother sins against you, rebuke him. Go, show him his fault when the two of you are alone. If he listens to you and if he repents, forgive him. You have gained back your brother.

If he sins against you seven times in the day and seven times returns, saying, *I repent,* you shall forgive him.

But, if he does not listen, take one or two more with you, so that every word may be established at the mouth of two or three witnesses. If he refuses to listen to them, tell it to the assembly. If he also refuses to hear the assembly, let him be to you as a Gentile or a tax collector.

Truly I tell you, whatever things you bind on earth will be bound in heaven, and whatever things you release on earth will be released in heaven.

And truly I tell you, if two of you agree on earth about anything that they ask, it will be done for you by my Father in heaven.

Where two or three are gathered together in my name, I am there in the midst of them.

☙❦❧

Then Simon came and said to him, "Lord, how often shall I forgive my brother if he sins against me? Until seven times?"

Jesus said to him,

I do not tell you *until seven times,* but *until seventy times seven.*

The kingdom of heaven is like a certain king who wanted to reconcile accounts with his servants.

When he had begun to reconcile, one was brought to him who owed him ten thousand talents. But, because he could not pay, his lord commanded him to be sold – with his wife, his children, and all that he had – and payment to be made.

The servant fell down and knelt before him, saying, *Lord, have patience with me, and I will repay you all.* Being moved with compassion, the lord of that servant released him and forgave him the debt.

But that servant went out and found one of his fellow servants, who owed him one hundred denarii. He grabbed him and took him by the throat, saying, *Pay me what you owe.*

So his fellow servant fell down at his feet and begged him, saying, *Have patience with me, and I will repay you.* But he would not and went and cast him into prison, until he should pay back that which was due.

When his fellow servants saw what was done, they were greatly saddened, and they came and told their lord all that was done.

Then his lord called him in and said to him, *You wicked servant. I forgave you all that debt because you begged me. Should you not also have had mercy on your fellow servant, even as I had mercy on you?* The angry lord delivered him to the tormentors, until he should pay all that was due.

So my heavenly Father will also do to you if you do not each forgive your brother from your hearts for his misdeeds.

⁂

While they were staying in Galilee, Jesus said to his disciples, "The Son of Man is about to be delivered into the hands of others and they will kill him and, after he is killed, on the third day he will rise again."

But they did not understand this saying – it was concealed from them, so that they should not perceive it – and they were afraid to ask him. They were exceedingly sorry.

Part 11

FINAL JOURNEY

FINAL JOURNEY

An account of events related to
the final journey of Jesus the Messiah

Part 11

Jesus prepares for travel to Jerusalem

WHEN THE DAYS WERE near that he should be taken up, Jesus intently set his face toward Jerusalem and sent messengers ahead of him.

He appointed seventy others and sent them two by two into every city and place where he was about to come.

He said to them,

The harvest is indeed plentiful, but the laborers are few. Pray therefore to the Lord of the harvest, that he may send out laborers into his harvest.

Go your ways. Behold, I send you out as lambs among wolves. Carry no purse, no wallet, no sandals. Greet no one on the way. Whatever house you enter, first say, *Peace be to this house.* If anyone of peace is there, your peace will rest on that one but, if not, it will return to you.

Remain in that same house, eating and drinking the things they give, for the laborer is worthy of his wages. Do not go from house to house.

In whatever city you enter and they receive you, eat the things that are set before you. Heal the sick who are there, and tell them, *The kingdom of God has come near to you.*

In whatever city you enter and they do not receive you, go out into its streets and say, *Even the dust from your city that clings to us, we wipe off against you. Yet know this, the kingdom of God has come near to you.* I tell you, it will be more tolerable in that day for Sodom than for that city.

Then he began to denounce the cities in which most of his mighty works had been done, because they did not repent.

Woe to you, Chorazin. Woe to you, Bethsaida. For if the mighty works had been done in Tyre and Sidon which were done in you, they would have repented long ago, sitting in sackcloth and ashes. But I tell you, on the day of judgment it will be more tolerable for Tyre and Sidon than for you.

You, Capernaum, who are exalted to heaven, will be brought down to Hades. For if the mighty works had been done in Sodom which were done in you, it would have remained until this day. But I tell you, on the day of judgment it will be more tolerable for the land of Sodom than for you.

Whoever listens to you listens to me, and whoever rejects you rejects me. And whoever rejects me rejects him who sent me.

❀⟊❀

When the seventy returned, they did so with joy, saying, "Lord, even the demons are subject to us in your name."

Jesus said to them,

I saw Satan falling like lightning from heaven. Behold, I give you authority to tread on serpents and scorpions and over all the power of the enemy.

Nothing will in any way hurt you. Nevertheless, do not rejoice in this, that the spirits are subject to you, but rejoice that your names are written in heaven.

In that same hour Jesus rejoiced in the Holy Spirit and said,

I thank you, Father, Lord of heaven and earth, that you have hidden these things from the wise and understanding and have revealed them to little children – yes, Father, for so it was well-pleasing in your sight.

All things have been delivered to me by my Father. No one knows who the Son is, except the Father, and who the Father is, except the Son, and anyone to whom the Son desires to reveal him.

Turning to the disciples, Jesus said privately,

Blessed are the eyes that see the things that you see, for I tell you that many prophets and kings desired to see the things that you see and did not see them, and to hear the things that you hear and did not hear them.

✻❈✻

Behold, a lawyer stood up and tested him, saying, "Teacher, what shall I do to inherit eternal life?"

Jesus said to him, "What is written in the law? How do you read it?"

The man answered, "You shall love the Lord your God with all your heart, with all your soul, with all your strength, and with all your mind, and you shall love your neighbor as yourself."

Jesus said, "You have answered correctly. Do this, and you will live."

Desiring to justify himself, the lawyer asked Jesus, "Who is my neighbor?"

Jesus answered,

A certain man was going down from Jerusalem to Jericho, and he fell among robbers, who stripped him and beat him and departed, leaving him half dead.

By chance, a certain priest was going down that way and, when he saw him, he passed by on the other side. In the same way a

Levite also, when he came to the place and saw him, passed by on the other side.

But a certain Samaritan, as he traveled, came where the man was and, when he saw him, was moved with compassion. He came to him, poured oil and wine on his wounds, and bound them up. He set him on his own animal and brought him to an inn and took care of him.

The next day, when he departed, he took out two denarii, gave them to the host, and said to him, *Take care of him. Whatever you spend beyond that, I will repay you when I return.*

Now which of these three do you think seemed to be a neighbor to the one who fell among the robbers?

The lawyer said, "He who showed mercy on him."

Jesus said to him, "Go and do likewise."

Jesus makes way to Samaria

On his way to Jerusalem, Jesus was passing along the borders of Samaria and Galilee.

As he entered a village, ten lepers met him. They stood at a distance and lifted up their voices, saying, "Jesus, Master, have mercy on us."

When he saw them, he said to them, "Go and show yourselves to the priests." As they went, they were cleansed.

One of them, when he saw that he was healed, turned back, glorifying God with a loud voice. He fell on his face at Jesus' feet, giving him thanks. He was a Samaritan.

Jesus asked, "Were not ten cleansed? Where are the nine? Were there none found who returned to give glory to God, except this stranger?"

Then he said to the Samaritan, "Get up and go your way. Your faith has healed you."

❧❀❧

Along the way, Jesus was asked by the Pharisees when the kingdom of God would come, and he answered them, "The kingdom of God does not come with observation – they will not say, 'Look, here,' or, 'Look, there' – for, behold, the kingdom of God is within you."

Then he said to the disciples,

The time will come when you will desire to see one of the days of the Son of Man, and you will not see it. They will tell you, *Look, here,* or, *Look, there.*

Do not go away nor follow after them – for as the lightning, when it flashes out of the one part under the sky, shines to the other part under the sky, so will the Son of Man be in his day. But first he must suffer many things and be rejected by this generation.

As it happened in the days of Noah, so will it be also in the days of the Son of Man. They ate, they drank, they married, they were given in marriage, until the day that Noah entered into the ship and the flood came and destroyed them all.

Likewise, as it happened in the days of Lot, they ate, they drank, they bought, they sold, they planted, they built – but, on the day that Lot went out from Sodom, it rained fire and sulfur from the sky and destroyed them all.

It will be the same on the day that the Son of Man is revealed. On that day, anyone who will be on the housetop with goods in the house should not go down to take them away. Anyone in the field should likewise not turn back.

Remember Lot's wife. Whoever seeks to save life loses it, but whoever loses life preserves it.

I tell you, on that night there will be two people in one bed. The one will be taken, and the other will be left. Two will be in the field, and the one will be taken and the other will be left. There will be two grinding grain together. One will be taken, and the other will be left.

The Pharisees asked him, "Where, Lord?"

And Jesus said to them, "Where the body is, there the vultures will also gather."

⁂

He also told them a parable, saying that they must always pray and not give up,

There was a judge in a certain city who did not fear God and did not respect man. A widow was in that city, and she often came to him, saying, *Defend me from my adversary.*

For a while he would not, but afterward he said to himself, *Though I neither fear God nor respect man, yet because this widow bothers me, I will defend her, or else she will wear me out by her continual coming.*

The Lord said,

Listen to what the unrighteous judge says.

Will God not avenge his chosen ones who cry out to him day and night? Will he yet exercise patience with them? I tell you that he will avenge them quickly.

Nevertheless, when the Son of Man comes, will he find faith on the earth?

He also told this parable for people who were convinced of their own righteousness and who despised all others,

Two men went into the temple to pray – one was a Pharisee, and the other was a tax collector.

The Pharisee stood and prayed to himself like this, *God, I thank you that I am not like the rest of men – extortionists, adulterers, the unrighteous, or even like this tax collector. I fast twice a week, and I give tithes of all that I get.*

But the tax collector, standing far away, would not even lift up his eyes to heaven, but instead beat his breast, saying, *God, be merciful to me, a sinner.*

Truly I tell you, this man went down to his house justified, rather than the other.

All who exalt themselves will be humbled, but all who humble themselves will be exalted.

They entered a village of the Samaritans, but they would not receive him, because he was traveling toward Jerusalem.

When his disciples James and John saw this, they said, "Lord, do you want us to command fire to come down from the sky and destroy them, just as Elijah did?"

He turned and rebuked them, "You do not know of what kind of spirit you are, for the Son of Man did not come to destroy lives, but to save them."

They went to another village.

Jesus proceeds to Judea

So Jesus traveled through cities and villages, teaching as he made his way to Jerusalem.

Someone asked him, "Lord, are they few who are saved?"

He said to them,

Strive to enter in by the narrow door, for many, I tell you, will seek to enter in and will not be able.

When once the master of the house has risen and shut the door, and you begin to stand outside and knock at the door, saying, *Lord, Lord, open to us,* then he will answer you, *I do not know you or where you come from.*

Then you will begin to say, *We ate and drank in your presence, and you taught in our streets.*

He will say, *I tell you, I do not know where you come from. Depart from me, all you workers of iniquity.*

There will be weeping and gnashing of teeth when you see Abraham, Isaac, Jacob, and all the prophets in the kingdom of God, and you yourselves are thrown outside. But people will come from the east, west, north, and south, and will sit down in the kingdom of God.

Behold, there are some who are last who will be first, and there are some who are first who will be last.

❈❈❈

Jesus came into the borders of Judea and beyond the Jordan. Great crowds came to him and, as he usually did, he again taught them and healed them there.

Some Pharisees came to him and, testing him, they asked, "Is it lawful for a man to divorce his wife for any reason?"

Jesus answered,

From the beginning of the creation, God made them male and female and said, *For this cause a man shall leave his father and mother and shall join to his wife, and the two shall become one flesh.* So they are no more two, but one flesh.

What therefore God has joined together, let no one tear apart.

They asked him, "Why then did Moses command us to give her a certificate of divorce and then divorce her?"

He said to them,

Because of the hardness of your hearts, Moses wrote this commandment allowing you to divorce your wives, but from the beginning it was not so.

I tell you that whoever divorces his wife, except for sexual immorality, and marries another, commits adultery, and he who marries her when she is divorced commits adultery.

Later, his disciples asked him again about the same matter.

He said to them,

Whoever divorces his wife and marries another commits adultery against her. If a woman herself divorces her husband and marries another, she commits adultery. And whoever marries one who is divorced from her husband commits adultery.

His disciples said to him, "If this is the case of the man with his wife, it is not expedient to marry."

But Jesus said,

Not everyone can receive this saying, but only those to whom it is given. There are eunuchs who were born that way from their mother's womb, and there are eunuchs who were made eunuchs by others, and there are eunuchs who made themselves eunuchs for the sake of the kingdom of heaven. Let anyone receive this who is able to receive it.

※ৠ೮ৡ✲

People brought little children to him, so that he would touch them and pray.

When the disciples saw it, they rebuked those who were bringing them.

But Jesus was moved with indignation. He summoned the disciples and said to them,

Allow the little children to come to me, and do not forbid them. The kingdom of God belongs to ones such as these. Truly I tell you, whoever will not receive the kingdom of God like a little child will in no way enter into it.

He took them in his arms and, laying his hands on them, blessed them.

※ৠ೮ৡ✲

As they went on their way, he entered into the village of Bethany, and a woman named Martha received him into her house.

She had a sister called Mary, who sat at Jesus' feet and heard his word. But Martha was distracted with much serving, and she came to him and said, "Lord, do you not care that my sister left me to serve alone? Ask her therefore to help me."

Jesus answered, "Martha, Martha, you are anxious and troubled about many things, but only one thing is needed. Mary has chosen the good part, which will not be taken away from her."

Jesus speaks of eternal life

He went away again beyond the Jordan to the place where John was baptizing at first, and there he stayed for some time.

Many came to him. They said, "John indeed did no sign, but everything that John said about this man is true." Many believed in him there.

✻ᘯᘔᘖ✻

As he was going back out on the journey, a man ran to him, knelt before him, and asked, "Good Teacher, what shall I do to inherit eternal life?"

Jesus said to him, "Why do you call me good? No one is good except one, that is, God. But, if you want to enter into life, keep the commandments. You shall not murder. You shall not commit adultery. You shall not steal. You shall not offer false testimony. Honor your father and mother, and love your neighbor as yourself."

The young man said, "I have observed all these things from my youth. What do I still lack?"

Jesus, looking at him, said, "You still lack one thing. If you want to be perfect, go, sell all that you have and give the money to the poor, and you will have treasure in heaven. Then come, follow me."

But when the young man heard these things, his face fell, and he went away sorrowful, for he was very rich and had great possessions.

⁂

Then Jesus said to his disciples, "How hard it is for those who have riches to enter into the kingdom of heaven. It is easier for a camel to enter through a needle's eye than for a rich man to enter the kingdom of God."

When the disciples heard this, they were exceedingly astonished and amazed at his words, and they said, "Who then can be saved?"

Jesus, looking at them, said, "The things which are impossible for people are possible with God. With God all things are possible."

Then Simon said, "Behold, we have left everything and followed you. What then will we have?"

Jesus said to them,

> **Truly I tell you, there is no one who has left house or wife or mother or father or brothers or sisters or children or land – for my sake or for the sake of the kingdom of God – who will not receive one hundred times more and inherit eternal life in the age to come.**

> **But many who are first will be last, and the last will be first.**

> **The kingdom of heaven is like the master of a household who went out early in the morning to hire laborers for his vineyard.**

When he had agreed with the laborers for a denarius a day, he sent them into his vineyard.

He went out about the third hour and saw others standing idle in the marketplace. To them he said, *You also go into the vineyard, and whatever is right I will give you.* So they went.

Again he went out about the sixth and the ninth hour and did likewise. About the eleventh hour, he went out and found others standing idle. He said to them, *Why do you stand here all day idle?*

They said to him, *Because no one has hired us.*

He said to them, *You also go into the vineyard, and you will receive whatever is right.*

When evening came, the lord of the vineyard said to his manager, *Call the laborers and pay them their wages, beginning from the last to the first.*

When those who were hired at about the eleventh hour came, they each received a denarius.

When the first came, they supposed that they would receive more, but they likewise each received a denarius.

When they received it, they murmured against the master of the household, saying, *These last have spent one hour, and you have made them equal to us who have borne the burden of the day and the scorching heat.*

But he answered one of them, *Friend, I am doing you no wrong. Did you not agree with me for a denarius? It is my desire to give to this last just as much as to you. Is it not lawful for me to do what I want with what I own? Or is your eye evil, because I am good? Take that which is yours, and go your way.*

So the last will be first, and the first will be last.

※✧❋✧※

Salome – the mother of James and John, the sons of Zebedee – came to Jesus with her sons and, kneeling, asked a certain thing of him.

He said to her, "What do you want me to do?"

She said to him, "Grant that these, my two sons, may sit – one at your right hand and one at your left hand – in your kingdom of glory."

Jesus answered, "You do not know what you are asking." To the sons, he said, "Are you able to drink the cup that I drink and be baptized with the baptism with which I am baptized?"

They replied, "We are able."

Jesus then said, "You will indeed drink my cup and be baptized with the baptism with which I am baptized. But the seat at my right hand or at my left hand is not mine to give – it is given to the one for whom my Father has prepared it."

When the ten heard it, they were indignant with the two brothers.

But Jesus summoned them and said,

You know that the rulers of the nations lord it over them, and their great ones exercise authority over them. But it shall not be so among you.

Whoever desires to become great among you shall be your servant, and whoever of you desires to become first among you shall be bondservant of all – even as the Son of Man came not to be served but to serve, and to give his life as a ransom for many.

Jesus returns to Judea

Lazarus – the brother of Martha and her sister Mary, from the village of Bethany – was sick. The sisters therefore sent a message to Jesus, saying, "Lord, behold, he for whom you have great affection is sick."

But when Jesus heard it, he said, "This sickness does not cause death. It is but for the glory of God, so that God's Son may be glorified by it."

So, though Jesus loved Martha and her sister and Lazarus, Jesus stayed two days in the place where he was after he heard that Lazarus was sick.

✻✽✾✿✻

Then, after this, he said to the disciples, "Let us go into Judea again."

The disciples told him, "Rabbi, the Jews were just trying to stone you, and you are going there again?"

Jesus answered, "Are there not twelve hours of daylight? Those who walk in the day do not stumble, because they see the light of this world. But those who walk in the night stumble, because the light is not in them."

After that, he said to them, "Our friend, Lazarus, has fallen asleep, but I am going so that I may wake him out of sleep."

The disciples said, "Lord, if he has fallen asleep, he will recover."

Now Jesus had spoken of his death, but they thought that he spoke of taking rest in sleep. So Jesus then said to them plainly, "Lazarus is dead. I am glad for your sake that I was not there, so that you may believe. Nevertheless, let us go to him."

Thomas, who is called Didymus, said to his fellow disciples, "Let us go also, that we may die with him."

❦

As Jesus, with his disciples and a great crowd, came near Jericho, a blind beggar – Bartimaeus, the son of Timaeus – was sitting by the road. Hearing the crowd going by, he asked what this meant.

They told him that Jesus of Nazareth was passing by.

When he heard this, he cried out, "Jesus, son of David, have mercy on me."

Many rebuked him to be quiet, but he cried out much more, "Have mercy on me, Lord, you son of David."

Jesus stood still and commanded the man to be brought to him, and they called the blind man, saying to him, "Take heart. Get up. He is calling you."

Casting away his cloak, the blind man sprang up and came to Jesus. When he had come near, Jesus asked him, "What do you want me to do for you?"

He said, "Lord, let it be that I may see again."

Moved with compassion, Jesus touched his eyes and said to him, "Receive your sight. Your faith has made you well."

Immediately, he received his sight and followed him, glorifying God. All the people, when they saw it, praised God.

❧

Then Jesus entered Jericho and was passing through it.

A man was there named Zacchaeus. He was a chief tax collector, and he was rich. He was trying to see who Jesus was but could not see over the crowd because he was short. He ran on ahead and climbed up a sycamore tree to see him, for Jesus was to pass that way.

When Jesus came to the place, he looked up and saw him, and said, "Zacchaeus, hurry and come down, for today I must stay at your house." Zacchaeus hurried down and received him joyfully.

When they saw it, the people murmured, saying, "He has gone to lodge with a man who is a sinner."

Zacchaeus stood and said to the Lord, "Behold, Lord, half of my goods I give to the poor. If I have wrongfully exacted anything of anyone, I will restore four times as much."

Jesus said to him, "Today, salvation has come to this house, because you also are a son of Abraham – for the Son of Man came to seek and to save that which was lost."

❧

As they listened to these things, Jesus went on and told a parable, because he was near Jerusalem and they supposed that the kingdom of God would be revealed immediately.

He said,

A nobleman went into a far country to get a kingdom for himself and then return. He called ten servants of his and gave them ten mina coins – one to each – and told them, *Conduct business until I come back.*

Now his citizens hated him and sent an envoy after him, saying, *We do not want this man to reign over us.*

When he came back, having received the kingdom, he called the servants to whom he had given the money, so that he might know what they had gained by conducting business.

One servant came before him, saying, *Lord, your mina has made ten more minas.* The nobleman said to him, *Well done, you good servant. Because you were found faithful with very little, you shall have authority over ten cities.*

Then another came, saying, *Your mina, Lord, has made five minas.* And the nobleman said to him, *You are to have authority over five cities.*

Then a third came, saying, *Lord, behold, your mina, which I kept laid away in a handkerchief, for I feared you, because you are an exacting man. You take up that which you did not lay down, and reap that which you did not sow.*

The nobleman said to him, *Out of your own mouth will I judge you, you wicked servant. You knew that I am an exacting man, taking up that which I did not lay down and reaping that which I did not sow. Then why did you not deposit my money in the bank so that, at my coming, I might have earned interest on it?*

He said to those who stood by, *Take the mina away from him, and give it to him who has the ten minas.*

They said to him, *Lord, he has ten minas.*

And he said, *I tell you that to everyone who has, more will be given, but from those who do not have much, even that which they have will be taken away. And – as to those enemies of mine who did not want me to reign over them here – bring them here and kill them before me.*

Jesus restores life to Lazarus

When Jesus arrived in Bethany, he found that Lazarus had already been in the tomb four days.

Now Bethany was near Jerusalem, about fifteen stadia away. Many of the Jews had joined the women around Martha and Mary, to console them about their brother.

When Martha heard that Jesus was coming, she went and met him, but Mary stayed in the house. Martha said to Jesus, "Lord, if you had been here, my brother would not have died. Even now I know that God will give you whatever you ask of him."

Jesus said to her, "Your brother will rise again."

Martha said to him, "I know that he will rise again in the resurrection on the last day."

Jesus said to her, "I am the resurrection and the life. All who believe in me will still live, even if they die. Whoever lives and believes in me will never die. Do you believe this?"

She said to him, "Yes, Lord. I have come to believe that you are the Messiah, the Son of God – he who comes into the world."

༺ﻬ༻

When she had said this, she went away and called her sister Mary and said secretly, "The Teacher is here and is calling you." When she heard this, she arose quickly and went to him.

Now Jesus had not yet come into the village but was in the place where Martha met him. The Jews who were with her in the house consoling her saw Mary rise up quickly and go out. They followed her, saying, "She is going to the tomb to weep there."

When Mary came to where Jesus was and saw him, she fell down at his feet, saying to him, "Lord, if you had been here, my brother would not have died."

When Jesus saw her weeping, and the Jews who came with her weeping, he groaned in the spirit and was troubled. He said, "Where have you laid him?"

They told him, "Lord, come and see."

Jesus wept. So the Jews said, "See how much affection he had for him." But some of them said, "Could this man who opened the eyes of the man who was blind not also have kept this man from dying?"

❦

Jesus, again groaning in himself, came to the tomb. It was a cave, and a stone lay against it. Jesus said, "Take away the stone."

Martha said to him, "Lord, by this time there is a stench, for he has been dead four days."

Jesus said to her, "Did I not tell you that, if you believed, you would see God's glory?"

So they took away the stone.

Jesus lifted up his eyes, and said, "Father, I thank you that you listened to me. I know that you always listen to me, but I said this because of those who stand around, so that they may believe that you sent me."

When he had said this, he cried with a loud voice, "Lazarus, come out."

He who was dead came out, bound hand and foot with wrappings, and his face was wrapped around with a cloth. Jesus said to them, "Free him, and let him go."

Jesus makes approach to Jerusalem

After these things, he went on ahead, going up to Jerusalem. Those who followed were amazed and afraid.

While Jesus was on the way, he took the twelve disciples aside and said to them,

> **Behold, we are going to Jerusalem, and all the things that are written through the prophets concerning the Son of Man will be completed.**

> **The Son of Man will be delivered to the chief priests and scribes, and they will condemn him to death and will hand him over to the Gentiles, who will mock him, spit on him, scourge him, and kill him, and on the third day he will rise again.**

The meaning of this was hidden from them, and they did not understand the things that were said.

❦

As they approached Jerusalem — near Bethphage and Bethany, at the Mount of Olives — Jesus sent two of his disciples, saying to them, "Go into the village that is on the other side. Immediately as you enter, you will find tied there a young donkey, on which no one has sat. Untie it, and bring it here. If anyone asks, 'Why are you doing this?' say, 'The Lord needs it, but he will send it back.'"

They went away and found a young donkey tied at the door, outside in the open street. As they were untying the donkey, its owners asked them, "Why are you untying the colt?" They told them just as Jesus had said, and they let them go.

They brought the young donkey to Jesus and threw their garments on it, and Jesus sat on it.

A great crowd – aware that Jesus had called Lazarus out of the tomb and raised him from the dead – heard that Jesus was coming to Jerusalem and went out to meet him.

As he was now getting near, at the descent of the Mount of Olives, many spread their cloaks on the way, and others spread branches of palm trees and other branches cut down from the trees.

Those who went in front and those who followed began to rejoice and praise God and cried out with a loud voice, "Hosanna. Blessed is he who comes in the name of the Lord – the king of Israel. Blessed is the kingdom of our ancestor David coming in the name of the Lord. Hosanna, peace in heaven, and glory in the highest."

⁂

Some of the Pharisees from the crowd said to him, "Teacher, rebuke your disciples."

Jesus answered them, "I tell you that, if these were silent, the stones would cry out."

The Pharisees then said among themselves, "See how you accomplish nothing. Behold, the world has gone after him."

⁂

When Jesus drew near and saw the city, he wept over it, saying,

> If you, even you, had known today the things that belong to your peace ... but now they are hidden from your eyes.

> The days will come on you when your enemies will throw up a barricade against you, surround you, and hem you in on every side. They will dash you and your children within you to the ground, and they will not leave in you one stone on another, because you did not know the time of your visitation.

⁑☙⁑

When he came into Jerusalem, all the city was stirred up with people saying, "Who is this?" and the multitudes said, "This is the prophet, Jesus, from Nazareth of Galilee."

Part 12

JERUSALEM TEACHING

JERUSALEM
TEACHING

An account of events related to
the final teaching of Jesus the Messiah

Part 12

Jesus arrives in Jerusalem

WHEN JESUS FIRST ARRIVED in Jerusalem, he entered into the temple. When he had looked around at everything, it being now evening, he went out to the Mount of Olives, near Bethany, with the twelve.

⁂

In the morning, as he returned to the city, he was hungry. Seeing a fig tree afar off by the road, he came to see if perhaps he might find anything on it.

When he came to it, he found nothing on it but leaves, for it was not the season for figs. Jesus said to it, "Let there be no fruit from you forever." And the fig tree withered away from the roots immediately.

When the disciples saw it, they marveled, saying, "How did the fig tree wither away immediately?"

Jesus answered them,

Truly I tell you, if you have faith in God and do not doubt, not only will you do what was done to the fig tree but, even if you told this mountain, *Be taken up and cast into the sea,* it would be done.

If you do not doubt in your heart, but believe that what he says is happening, you shall have whatever he says.

Whatever you ask in prayer, believe that you will receive, and you shall have all things.

Whenever you stand praying, forgive anything you have against anyone, so that your Father in heaven may also forgive you your transgressions. If you do not forgive, neither will your Father in heaven forgive your transgressions.

Jesus teaches in the temple

On arrival in Jerusalem, Jesus entered the temple and began to drive out all those who bought and sold there.

He overthrew the tables of the money changers and the seats of those who sold the doves, and he would not allow anyone to carry a container through the temple.

He said to them, "It is written, 'My house shall be called a house of prayer for all the nations,' but you have made it a den of thieves."

※⚜※

Thereafter, every day, Jesus taught in the temple, and all the people came early in the morning to hear him there. Every night, he would go out to the Mount of Olives, opposite the temple, and spend the night.

※⚜※

One day, as he was teaching the people in the temple and proclaiming the good news, Jesus looked up and saw people putting their gifts into the treasury.

Many who were rich cast in much. Then a poor widow came, and she cast in two lepta – small brass coins which together equal a quadrans. He called his disciples and said to them, "Truly I tell you, this poor widow gave more than all those who are giving into the treasury. They all gave out of their abundance, but she gave out of her poverty and put in all that she had to live on."

Jesus speaks in parables

Jesus began to speak to the people in parables.

"What do you think? A man had two sons. He came to the first, and said, 'Son, go work today in my vineyard.' The son answered, 'I will not,' but afterward he changed his mind and went. The father came to the second son and said the same thing. The second answered, 'I go, sir,' but he did not go. Which of the two did the will of his father?"

They answered, "The first."

Jesus said to them, "Truly I tell you, the tax collectors and the prostitutes are entering into the kingdom of God before you. For John came to you in the way of righteousness and you did not believe him, but the tax collectors and the prostitutes believed him. When you saw it, you did not even repent afterward, so that you might believe him."

Then he told them other parables.

༺ﾟ❀ﾟ༻

A man, going to another country, called his own servants and entrusted his goods to them, to each according to his own ability. To one he gave five talents, to another two, and to another one. Then he went on his journey.

He who received the five talents immediately went and traded with them and made another five talents. In like manner, he who got the two gained another two. But he who received the one went away and dug in the earth and hid his lord's money.

After a long time, the lord of those servants came and reconciled accounts with them. He who received the five talents came and brought another five talents, saying, *Lord, you delivered to me five talents. Behold, I have gained another five talents besides them.* His lord said to him, *Well done, good and faithful servant. You have been faithful over a few things – I will set you over many things. Enter into the joy of your lord.*

He who got the two talents came and said, *Lord, you delivered to me two talents. Behold, I have gained another two talents besides them.* His lord said to him, *Well done, good and faithful servant. You have been faithful over a few things – I will set you over many things. Enter into the joy of your lord.*

He who had received the one talent came and said, *Lord, I knew you that you are a hard man, reaping where you did not sow and gathering where you did not scatter. I was afraid and went away and hid your talent in the earth. Behold, you have what is yours.*

But his lord answered him, *You wicked and slothful servant. You knew that I reap where I did not sow and gather where I did not scatter. You ought therefore to have deposited my money with the bankers and, at my coming I should have received back my own with interest. Take away the talent from him, and give it to the one who has the ten talents. To everyone who has, more will be given, and there will be abundance, but from those who do not have much, even that which they have will be taken away. Throw the unprofitable servant into the outer darkness, where there will be weeping and gnashing of teeth.*

※〜ᢙᠥ〜※

The kingdom of heaven will be like this. Ten virgins took their lamps and went out to meet the bridegroom. Five of them were foolish and took no oil with them, but five were wise and took oil in their vessels along with their lamps.

Now, as the bridegroom was delayed, they all slumbered and slept. But at midnight there was a cry, *Behold. The bridegroom is coming. Come out to meet him.*

All those virgins arose and trimmed their lamps. The foolish ones said to the wise, *Give us some of your oil, for our lamps are going out.*

But the wise ones answered, *What if there is not enough for us and you? You go rather to those who sell, and buy for yourselves.*

While they went away to buy, the bridegroom came, and those who were ready went in with him to the marriage feast, and the door was shut. Afterward the other virgins also came, saying, *Lord, Lord, open to us.* But he answered, *I do not know you.*

Watch, therefore, for you do not know the day nor the hour in which the Son of Man is coming.

❧❀❧

There was a master of a household, who planted a vineyard, set a hedge about it, dug a pit for the winepress, and built a tower. Then he leased it out to farmers and went to another country for a long time.

When the season for the fruit drew near, he sent a servant to the farmers to get his share of the fruit of the vineyard. But they took him, beat him, and sent him away empty.

He sent another servant to them, and they threw stones at him, wounded him in the head, and sent him away shamefully treated. Again he sent another, and they killed him. And so it was with many others – some were beaten, some were killed.

Still having one, his beloved son, he sent his son to them, saying, *They will respect my son.* But, when the farmers saw the son, they reasoned among themselves, saying, *This is the heir. Come, let us kill him, and the inheritance may be ours.* So they took him, killed him, and threw him out of the vineyard.

When the lord of the vineyard comes, what will he do to those farmers? He will miserably destroy those miserable men and will lease out the vineyard to other farmers, who will give him the fruit in its season.

Have you not even read this scripture, *The stone that the builders rejected was made the chief cornerstone. This was from the Lord – it is marvelous in our eyes?*

Everyone who falls on this stone will be broken to pieces, and it will crush to dust anyone on whom it falls. Therefore I tell you, the kingdom of God will be taken away from you and given to a nation bringing forth its fruit.

When the chief priests, the scribes, and the Pharisees heard this last parable, they perceived that he had spoken it against them. They sought to lay hands on him that very hour, but they feared the people, because they considered him to be a prophet. So they left him and went away.

Leaders question the authority of Jesus

The blind and the lame came to him in the temple, and he healed them.

When the chief priests, the scribes, and the elders saw the wonderful things that he did and heard the children crying in the temple, saying, "Hosanna to the son of David," they were indignant and said to him, "Do you hear what these are saying?"

Jesus said to them, "Yes. Did you never read, 'Out of the mouth of babes and nursing babies you have perfected praise'?"

They asked him, "By what authority do you do these things? Who gave you this authority?"

Jesus answered them, "I will ask you one question and, if you can answer, I will likewise tell you by what authority I do these things. The baptism of John — where was it from, from heaven or from the people?"

They reasoned with themselves, saying, "If we say, 'From heaven,' he will ask us, 'Why then did you not believe him?' But if we say, 'From the people,' the crowd will stone us, for they are persuaded that John was a prophet."

They answered Jesus, "We do not know." Then Jesus said to them, "Neither will I tell you by what authority I do these things."

The chief priests, the scribes, and the elders of the people sought how they might destroy him, for they feared him. But they could not find what they might do, for all the people were astonished at his teaching and hung on to every word he said.

Pharisees seek to entrap Jesus

The Pharisees went and took counsel on how they might entrap Jesus in his talk so as to deliver him up to the power and authority of the governor.

They sent their disciples to him, along with the Herodians. They pretended to be righteous when they said, "Teacher, we know that you are honest and do not defer to anyone. You are not partial to anyone but truly teach the way of God. Tell us, therefore, what do you think? Is it lawful to pay taxes to Caesar, or not? Shall we give, or shall we not give?"

But Jesus perceived their wickedness and hypocrisy and said, "Why do you test me? Show me the tax money." And they brought him a denarius.

He asked them, "Whose is this image and inscription?" They answered, "Caesar's."

Then he said to them, "Give therefore to Caesar the things that are Caesar's and to God the things that are God's."

When they heard this, they marveled greatly, and they were not able to trap him in his words before the people. They were silent and went away.

Jesus silences the Sadducees and Pharisees

That same day, some Sadducees – those who deny that there is a resurrection – came to him to ask a question. They said,

"Teacher, Moses wrote to us that, 'If a man's brother dies and leaves a wife behind him and leaves no children, his brother should take his wife and raise up offspring in his stead.'

"Now there were seven brothers. The first married and died and, having no seed, left his wife to his brother. The second took her and died, leaving no children behind him. In like manner the third took her, and likewise to the seventh. The seven all died and left no children.

"Afterward the woman also died. Therefore, in the resurrection, when they rise, whose wife will she be, for the seven all had her as a wife?"

Jesus said to them,

You are badly mistaken and do not know the scriptures nor the power of God. The children of this age marry and are given in marriage. But those who are considered worthy to attain to that age and the resurrection from the dead neither marry nor are given in marriage. They are like the angels in heaven and, being children of the resurrection, they are children of God.

Concerning the resurrection of the dead, even Moses showed at the bush that the dead are raised. God spoke to him, saying, *I am the God of Abraham, the God of Isaac, and the God of Jacob.* He is not the God of the dead, but of the living, for all are alive to him.

Some of the Sadducees answered, "Teacher, you speak well," and they did not dare to ask him any more questions.

※※※

But, when the Pharisees heard that he had silenced the Sadducees, they gathered together. They decided that one of them, a lawyer, would ask another question to test him.

He asked, "Teacher, which commandment in the law is the greatest of all?"

Jesus answered,

You shall love the Lord your God with all your heart, with all your soul, and with all your mind. This is the first and greatest commandment. And the second is like this – *You shall love your neighbor as yourself.*

There is no other commandment greater than these. On these two commandments the whole law and the prophets depend.

One scribe said to Jesus, "Teacher, you have said truly that he is the one, and there is none other but he. You have said well that to love him with all the heart – with all the understanding, with all the soul, and with all the strength – and to love one's neighbor as oneself are more important than all whole burnt offerings and sacrifices."

When Jesus saw that he spoke wisely, he said to him, "You are not far from the kingdom of God."

※※※

Now while the Pharisees were gathered together, Jesus asked them this question, "What do you think of the Messiah? Whose son is he?" They said to him, "The son of David."

He said to them,

How is it the scribes say that the Messiah is the son of David when David calls him *Lord?* David himself, in the Holy Spirit, said, *The Lord said to my Lord, 'Sit at my right hand, until I make your enemies the footstool for your feet.'* If David thus calls him *Lord,* how can he be his son?

The crowd heard Jesus gladly, and no one was able to answer. From that day forth, no one dared to ask him any more questions.

Jesus chastises the scribes and Pharisees

In the hearing of all the people, Jesus said to his disciples,

The scribes and the Pharisees sit on the seat of Moses. Therefore, observe whatever they tell you to observe, but do not do their works, for they say and do not. They bind heavy burdens that are grievous to be borne and lay them on the shoulders of others, but they themselves will not lift a finger to help them.

They do all their works to be seen by others. They make their phylacteries broad and enlarge the fringes of their garments.

They love to walk in long robes and to get salutations in the marketplaces, the places of honor at feasts, and the best seats in the synagogues. Beware of the scribes. They devour widows' houses and, for a pretense, make long prayers, and they like to be called *Rabbi.* But they will receive greater condemnation.

But you are not to be called *Rabbi,* for one is your teacher – the Messiah – and all of you are students. Neither be called masters, for one is your master – the Messiah. And call no man on earth your father, for one is your Father – he who is in heaven.

The greatest among you will be your servant. All who exalt themselves will be humbled, and all who humble themselves will be exalted.

Then Jesus said to the crowds,

But woe to you, scribes and Pharisees – hypocrites – because you shut up the kingdom of heaven against others. You do not enter in yourselves and, when others are entering, you do not allow them.

Woe to you, scribes and Pharisees – hypocrites – for you travel around by sea and land to make one convert and then make the convert twice as much a child of hell as yourselves.

Woe to you, blind guides, who say, *Whoever swears by the temple is not bound, but whoever swears by the gold of the temple is obligated.*

You blind fools, for which is greater – the gold or the temple that sanctifies the gold?

And you say, *Whoever swears by the altar is not bound, but whoever swears by the gift that is on it is obligated?*

You blind fools, for which is greater – the gift or the altar that sanctifies the gift? Whoever swears by the altar, swears by it and by everything on it. Whoever swears by the temple, swears by it and by him who is living in it. Whoever swears by heaven, swears by the throne of God and by him who sits on it.

Woe to you, scribes and Pharisees – hypocrites – for you tithe mint, dill, and cumin, and have left undone the weightier matters of the law – justice, mercy, and faith. You ought to have done these but ought not to have left the others undone. You blind guides, you strain out a gnat and swallow a camel.

Woe to you, scribes and Pharisees – hypocrites – for you clean the outside of the cup, but within it is full of extortion and self-indulgence. You blind Pharisees, first clean the inside of the cup, so that its outside may also become clean.

Woe to you, scribes and Pharisees – hypocrites – for you are like whitened tombs, which outwardly appear beautiful but inwardly are full of dead men's bones and all uncleanness. Even so, you also outwardly appear righteous to others, but inwardly you are full of hypocrisy and iniquity.

Woe to you, scribes and Pharisees – hypocrites – for you build the tombs of the prophets and decorate the tombs of the righteous, and say, *If we had lived in the days of our forebears, we would not have partaken with them in the blood of the prophets.*

Therefore, you testify to yourselves that you are children of those who killed the prophets. Fill up, then, the measure of your forebears. You serpents, you offspring of vipers, how will you escape the judgment of hell?

Therefore, behold, I send to you prophets, wise men, and scribes – some of whom you will kill and crucify, and some you will scourge in your synagogues and persecute from city to city – so that on you may come all the righteous blood shed on the earth, from the blood of righteous Abel to the blood of Zachariah, son of Barachiah, whom you killed between the sanctuary and the altar.

Truly I tell you, all these things will come upon this generation.

When the crowd heard all this, they were astonished at his teaching.

༺❄༻

Some Pharisees came to Jesus and said to him, "Get out of here and go away, for Herod wants to kill you."

He said to them,

Jerusalem, Jerusalem – the city that kills the prophets and stones those who are sent to her. How often I wanted to gather your children together, like a hen gathers her own brood under her wings, and you refused.

Behold, your house is left to you desolate. And, I tell you, you will not see me from now on, until you say, *Blessed is he who comes in the name of the Lord.*

Go and tell that fox that, behold, I cast out demons and perform cures today and tomorrow, and on the third day I complete my mission. Nevertheless I must go on my way – today and tomorrow and the next day – for it cannot be that a prophet perishes outside of Jerusalem.

※ぶぶ※

When evening came, he left them and went out of the city to the Mount of Olives and lodged there.

Jesus speaks on the Mount of Olives

One day, some were talking about the temple – how it was decorated with beautiful stones and gifts – when Jesus came out.

As he was going on his way, he said to his disciples, "Do you not see all of these buildings of the temple? Truly I tell you, as for these things that you see, the days will come when not one stone will be left on another. All will be thrown down."

※ぶぶ※

Later, as Jesus sat on the Mount of Olives, the disciples came to him and asked him privately, "When will these things be? What is the sign that the end of the age is about to happen? What is the sign of your coming?"

Jesus answered them,

The good news of the kingdom will be proclaimed in the whole world, as a testimony to all the nations, and then the end will come. But no one knows the day and hour, not even the angels in heaven nor the Son. Only the Father knows.

As the days of Noah were, so will be the coming of the Son of Man. In those days, before the flood, they were eating and drinking, marrying and giving in marriage, until the day Noah entered the ship. They did not know until the flood came and took them all away. So, too, will be the coming of the Son of Man. Then, of two in the field, one will be taken and one will be left.

So I tell you all, be watchful all the time. When you hear of wars and disturbances, do not be troubled. Nation will rise against nation, and kingdom will rise against kingdom. There will be great earthquakes in various places, there will be famines and plagues, there will be terrors and great signs from heaven. These things must happen first, but the end is not yet – all these things are but the beginning of birth pains.

After the oppression of those days, the sun will be darkened, and the moon will not give its light. The stars will fall from heaven, and nations will be in perplexity by the roaring of the sea and the waves. People will faint from fear and from expectation of the things coming on the world, for the powers of the heavens will be shaken.

It will come like a snare on all those who dwell on the surface of the earth, and many will stumble. They will deliver up one another and hate one another. Many false messiahs and false prophets will arise and show great signs and wonders, and they will lead many astray. Because iniquity will be multiplied, the love of many will grow cold. But the one who endures to the end will be saved.

Watch out that you do not get led astray. Many will come in my name, saying, *I am the Messiah,* and, *The time is at hand,* to lead even the chosen ones astray, if possible.

If any tell you, *Behold, here is the Messiah,* do not follow them. If they tell you, *Behold, he is in the wilderness,* do not go out. If they say, *Behold, he is in the inner chambers,* do not believe it. As the lightning flashes from the east and is seen even to the west, so will be the coming of the Son of Man. Wherever the carcass is, there the vultures gather.

Keep alert, for you do not know when the time is. Be careful that your hearts are not loaded down with carousing, drunkenness, and cares of this life. Beware that the day does not come on you suddenly. Know this – if the master of the house had known in what watch of the night the thief was coming, he would have watched and would not have allowed his house to be broken into. Therefore, also be ready, for the Son of Man will come in an hour that you do not expect.

It is like a man traveling to another country, having left his house and given authority to his servants and to each one his work and commanded the doorkeeper to keep watch. You do not know when the lord of the house is coming – at evening or at midnight or when the rooster crows or in the morning – so watch lest, coming suddenly, he might find you sleeping.

Blessed is the servant whom his lord finds at work when he comes. Truly I tell you, it is the faithful and wise servant whom his lord has set over his household to give them their portion of food at the right times.

But if that servant says in his heart, *My lord delays his coming,* and begins to beat the menservants and the maidservants and to eat and drink and be drunken, the lord will ascertain. He will come on a day when the servant does not expect it, at an hour that he does not know, and will cut him in two and place his portion with the unfaithful, where there will be weeping and gnashing of teeth.

The servant who knew his lord's will but did not prepare or do what he wanted will be beaten with many stripes. But the one who did not know what was wanted and did things worthy of stripes will be beaten with few stripes. From one to whom much is given, much will be required. From one to whom much was entrusted, even more will be asked.

But when you see Jerusalem surrounded by armies, then know that its desolation is at hand. And, when you see the abomination of desolation standing in the holy place, where it ought not be, then those in Judea must flee to the mountains, those who are in the midst of her must depart, and those in the country must not enter therein. These are days of vengeance.

The one on the housetop must not enter in to take anything out of his house. The one in the field must not return back to take his cloak. And woe to those who are pregnant and to those who nurse infants in those days, for there will be great distress in the land and wrath to this people. They will fall by the edge of the sword and be led captive into all the nations. Jerusalem will be trampled down by the Gentiles, until the times of the Gentiles are fulfilled.

Pray that the flight will not be in the winter, for there will be oppression in those days, such as has not been from the beginning of the world until now and never will be again. But for the sake of the chosen ones, whom the Lord has picked out, those days will be shortened and, unless those days are shortened, no flesh would be saved.

Watch yourselves and pray that you may be counted worthy to escape all these things that will happen and to stand before the Son of Man. The good news must first be proclaimed to all the nations. But in time they will lay their hands on you and persecute you, then they will deliver you up to oppression. You will be brought before kings and governors for my sake, to give testimony to them.

When they lead you away and deliver you up, do not be anxious about how or what you will say. Say whatever will be given you in that hour, for it is not you who will speak, but the Spirit of your Father who speaks in you.

I will give you a mouth and wisdom which all your adversaries will not be able to withstand or to contradict, although you will be hated by all for my name's sake. You will be handed over even by parents, brothers, relatives, and friends. And they will put you to death, but not a hair of your head will perish. By your endurance you will win your lives.

When these things begin to happen, look up and lift up your heads, because your redemption is near. From the fig tree learn this – when the branch becomes tender and puts forth its leaves, you know that the summer is near.

So also, when you see these things coming to pass, you know that kingdom of God is near, even at the doors.

The sign of the Son of Man will appear in the sky. Then all the tribes of the earth will mourn, and they will see the Son of Man coming in clouds with power and great glory. He will send out his angels with a great sound of a trumpet to gather together his chosen ones from the four winds, from the ends of the earth to the ends of the sky. When the Son of Man comes, and all the angels with him, he will sit on the throne of his glory.

All the nations will be gathered, and he will separate them one from another as a shepherd separates the sheep from the goats – he will set the sheep at his right hand and the goats at the left.

The king will tell those at his right hand, *Come, blessed of my Father, inherit the kingdom prepared for you from the foundation of the world. I was hungry, and you gave me food to eat. I was thirsty, and you gave me drink. I was a stranger, and you took me in. I was naked, and you clothed me. I was sick, and you visited me. I was in prison, and you came to me.*

And the righteous will ask, *Lord, when did we see you hungry and feed you, or thirsty and give you a drink? When did we see you as a stranger and take you in, or naked and clothe you? When did we see you sick or in prison and come to you?* The king will answer, *Truly I tell you, just as you did it to one of the least of these my brothers, you did it to me.*

Then he will say to those at the left hand, *Depart from me, you cursed, into the eternal fire that is prepared for the devil and his angels. I was hungry, and you did not give me food to eat. I was thirsty, and you gave me no drink. I was a stranger, and you did not take me in. I was naked, and you did not clothe me. I was sick and in prison, and you did not visit me.*

Then they will also ask, *Lord, when did we see you hungry, or thirsty, or a stranger, or naked, or sick, or in prison, and did not help you?* He will answer them, *Just as you did not do it to one of the least of these my brothers, you did not do it to me.* And they will go away into eternal punishment. The righteous will go into eternal life.

Truly I tell you, this generation will not pass away until all these things happen. Heaven and earth will pass away, but not my words. My words will not pass away.

Part 13

BETRAYAL

BETRAYAL

An account of events related to
the betrayal of Jesus the Messiah

Part 13

Jesus speaks to the Greeks

NOW THE PASSOVER OF the Jews was at hand, and many went up from the country to Jerusalem before the Passover to purify themselves. They sought Jesus and spoke with one another, as they stood in the temple, "What do you think? That he is not coming to the feast at all?"

❦

Now there were certain Greeks among those who went up to worship at the feast. They came to Philip, who was from Bethsaida of Galilee, and said to him, "Sir, we want to see Jesus."

Philip came and told Andrew and, in turn, Andrew came with Philip, and they told Jesus. Jesus spoke to them,

The time has come for the Son of Man to be glorified. Truly I tell you, unless a grain of wheat falls into the earth and dies, it remains by itself alone. But, if it dies, it bears much fruit.

Those who love life will lose it. Those who hate life in this world will keep it to eternal life. Anyone who serves me must follow me. Where I am, there will my servant also be. The Father will honor anyone who serves me.

Now my soul is troubled. What shall I say – *Father, save me from this time?* But I came to this time for this cause. Father, glorify your name.

Then there came a voice out of the sky,

I have glorified it and will glorify it again.

The crowd, who stood by and heard it, said that it had thundered. Others said, "An angel has spoken to him." Jesus answered,

This voice has not come for my sake, but for yours. Now is the judgment of this world. Now the prince of this world will be cast out. And, if I am lifted up from the earth, I will draw all people to myself.

The crowd answered him, "We have heard out of the law that the Messiah remains forever. How do you say, 'The Son of Man must be lifted up?' Who is this Son of Man?"

Jesus said to them,

The light is with you yet a little while. Walk while you have the light, so that darkness does not overtake you. If you walk in the darkness, you do not know where you are going.

While you have the light, believe in the light, so that you may become children of light.

✤

After Jesus said these things, he departed and hid from them.

Though he had done so many signs before them, they did not yet believe in him. Nevertheless many – even of the rulers – believed in him, but because of the Pharisees they did not confess it, so that they would not be put out of the synagogue. They loved praise from others more than God's praise.

The death of Jesus is planned

While many of the Jews who saw what Jesus did believed in him, some of them went to the Pharisees and told them the things that Jesus had done.

The chief priests, the scribes, the Pharisees, and the elders of the people came together in the court of the high priest, Caiaphas, and gathered a council.

They said, "What are we doing? This man does many signs. If we leave him alone like this, everyone will believe in him, and the Romans will come and take away both our place and our nation."

Caiaphas said to them, "You know nothing at all, nor do you consider that it is advantageous for us that one man should die for the people and that the whole nation shall not perish."

Now he did not say this of himself but, being high priest that year, he prophesied that Jesus would die for the nation, and not for the nation only, but that he might also gather together into one the children of God who are scattered abroad.

So from that day forward they took counsel on how they might put him to death – how they might take Jesus by deceit and kill him. But they said, "Not during the feast, lest a riot occur among the people."

※⁓⁀⁓※

Jesus therefore no longer walked openly among the Jews, but departed from there to a city called Ephraim in the country near the wilderness. He stayed there with his disciples.

Mary of Bethany anoints Jesus

Six days before the Passover, Jesus was in Bethany, in the house of Lazarus, whom Jesus raised from the dead. They made him a supper there. Martha served, and Lazarus was one of those who sat at the table with him.

As Jesus sat at the table, a woman, Mary, came to him with an alabaster jar of very precious ointment, made of pure nard. She broke the jar and poured it over his head. Then she anointed his feet and wiped them with her hair. The house was filled with the fragrance of the ointment.

When his disciples saw this, they were indignant, saying, "Why has this ointment been wasted?"

Judas Iscariot – who had the money box and used to steal what was put into it – said, "Why was this ointment not sold for three hundred denarii and the money given to the poor?"

But Jesus said to them,

> Leave her alone. Why do you trouble the woman? She has kept this for the day of my burial, and she has done a good work for me.
>
> You always have the poor with you and, whenever you want to, you can do them good. But you will not always have me.
>
> She has done what she could. In pouring this ointment on my body, she prepared me for burial. Truly I tell you – wherever this good news is proclaimed in the whole world – what this woman has done will also be spoken of as a memorial of her.

※≼⊱⊰≽※

A large crowd of Jews learned that he was there, and they came, not only for the sake of Jesus, but also that they might see Lazarus.

The chief priests conspired to put Lazarus to death also, because on account of him many of the Jews went away and believed in Jesus.

Judas Iscariot agrees to betray Jesus

Now it was two days before the feast of the Passover and the unleavened bread, and the chief priests and the scribes and the Pharisees sought how they might put Jesus to death, for they feared the people. They had commanded that anyone who knew where he was should report it, so that they might seize him.

❧

At this time, Jesus was with his disciples, and he cried out,

Whoever believes in me believes not in me but in him who sent me. Whoever sees me sees him who sent me.

I have come as a light into the world, so that whoever believes in me may not remain in the darkness. I do not judge anyone who listens to my sayings and does not believe, for I came not to judge the world, but to save the world.

The one who rejects me and does not receive my sayings has one who judges him. On the last day, the word that I spoke will be the judge, for I spoke not from myself, but the Father who sent me gave me a commandment about what I should say and what I should speak. I know that his commandment is eternal life. Therefore, I speak even as the Father has said to me.

When Jesus had finished all these words, he said to his disciples, "You know that after two days the Passover is coming, and the Son of Man will be delivered up to be crucified."

❧

It then happened that Satan entered into Judas Iscariot, who was one of the twelve, and he went away to the chief priests to talk about how he might deliver Jesus to them. He said, "What are you willing to give me if I should deliver him to you?"

When they heard this, they were glad, and they weighed out thirty pieces of silver for him. From that time, he sought opportunity to betray Jesus in the absence of a crowd.

Jesus and disciples share the Passover

On the first day of unleavened bread, when they sacrificed the Passover, Jesus said to Simon and John, "Go and prepare the Passover for us, so that we may eat."

They asked him, "Where do you want us to go and make ready?"

He said, "Go into the city, and there you will meet a man carrying a pitcher of water. Follow him into the house that he enters, and tell the master of the house, 'The Teacher says to you, "Where is the guest room where I may eat the Passover with my disciples?"' He will show you a large upper room, furnished and ready. Make preparations there."

The disciples did as Jesus commanded them and found things as he had told them, and they prepared the Passover.

❦

When evening had come, he reclined at the table with the twelve disciples.

He said to them, "I have earnestly desired to eat this Passover with you before I suffer – for I tell you, I will no longer eat of it until it is fulfilled in the kingdom of God."

As they were eating, Jesus took bread and, after he gave thanks and blessed it, he broke it and gave it to them and said,

Take. Eat. This is my body, which is given for you. Do this in memory of me.

Likewise he took a cup and, when he had given thanks, he gave to them and said,

Take this, and all of you drink it. This is my blood of the new covenant, which is poured out for many for the remission of sins.

Truly I tell you, I will no more drink of this fruit of the vine until that day when I drink it anew with you in the kingdom of God.

You are those who have continued with me in my trials. I confer on you – even as my Father conferred on me – a kingdom, so that you may eat and drink at my table in my kingdom.

In the regeneration, when the Son of Man sits on the throne of his glory, you who have followed me will also sit on twelve thrones, judging the twelve tribes of Israel.

Now the Son of Man has been glorified, and God has been glorified in him. God will also glorify him in himself and will glorify him immediately.

Little children, I will be with you a little while longer. You will seek me and as I said to the Jews, where I am going, you cannot come.

※ぐや৫※

After supper, Jesus – knowing that the Father had given all things into his hands and that he came forth from God and was going to God – arose from the table and laid aside his outer garments and wrapped a towel around his waist. Then he poured water into the basin and began to wash the disciples' feet and to wipe them with the towel.

He came to Simon, who said to him, "Lord, do you wash my feet?"

Jesus answered, "You do not know what I am doing now, but you will understand later."

Simon said to him, "You will never wash my feet."

Jesus replied, "If I do not wash you, you have no part with me."

Simon said to him, "Lord, not my feet only, but also my hands and my head."

Jesus said, "Someone who has bathed only needs to have his feet washed, then is completely clean. You are clean, but not all of you are clean."

When he had washed their feet, he put his outer garment back on and sat down again, and he said to them,

Do you know what I have done to you? You call me *Teacher* and *Lord*. You say so correctly, for so I am. If I then, the Lord and the Teacher, have washed your feet, you also ought to wash one another's feet. I have given you an example, so that you also should do as I have done to you.

Truly I tell you, a servant is not greater than his lord, neither is one sent greater than the one who sent him. If you know these things, blessed are you if you do them.

I do not speak about all of you – I know whom I have chosen – but so that the scripture may be fulfilled, *He who eats bread with me has lifted up his heel against me.*

I tell you before it happens, so that, when it happens, you may believe that I am he. Truly I tell you, whoever receives one whom I send receives me, and whoever receives me receives him who sent me.

❧⟐❧

When Jesus had said this, he was troubled in spirit and, as they sat and were eating, he testified, "Truly I tell you, one of you who eats with me will betray me – his hand is on the table."

The disciples looked at one another, perplexed about whom he spoke. They began to question among themselves which of them it was who would do this thing. They were exceedingly sorrowful, and each began to ask him, "It is not I, is it, Lord?"

One of his disciples, whom Jesus loved, was at the table, leaning against Jesus, and Simon beckoned to him and said, "Tell us who it is of whom he speaks." So, leaning back as he was, he asked Jesus, "Lord, who is it?"

Jesus answered them, "It is one of the twelve who dip with me in the dish. The Son of Man goes as it is written about him, but woe to that man through whom the Son of Man is betrayed. It would be better for that man if he had not been born."

Judas, in whose heart the devil had put the will to betray him, said, "It is not I, is it, Rabbi?"

Jesus answered, "It is he to whom I give this piece of bread when I have dipped it." When he had dipped the piece of bread, he gave it to Judas Iscariot, son of Simon.

After Judas received the piece of bread Jesus said to him, "What you do, do quickly."

Now no one at the table knew why Jesus said this to him. Some thought that, because Judas had the money box, Jesus was saying to him, "Buy what we need for the feast," or that he should give something to the poor. But Judas immediately went out into the night.

Jesus enlightens his disciples

After Judas left, a contention arose among the disciples regarding which of them was considered to be greatest.

Jesus said to them,

The kings of the nations lord it over them, and those who have authority over them are called benefactors. But not so with you. The one who is the greater among you should become as the younger, and one who is governing should become as one who serves.

For who is greater – one who sits at the table or one who serves? Is it not the one who sits at the table? But I am in the midst of you as one who serves.

Jesus then said to the disciples,

I am the way, the truth, and the life. No one comes to the Father except through me. If you had known me, you would have known my Father also. From now on, you know him and have seen him.

I am the true vine, and my Father is the farmer. He takes away every branch in me that does not bear fruit, and he prunes every branch that bears fruit, so that it may bear more fruit.

I am the vine. You are the branches, and you are already pruned clean because of the word that I have spoken to you.

Remain in me, and I in you. As the branch cannot bear fruit by itself unless it remains in the vine, so neither can you unless you remain in me. Those who remain in me, and I in them, bear much fruit, for apart from me they can do nothing.

Anyone who does not remain in me is thrown out as a branch and is withered. Branches such as these are gathered, thrown into the fire, and burned.

If you remain in me, and my words remain in you, you will ask whatever you desire, and it will be done for you. In this my Father is glorified – that you bear much fruit, and so you will be my disciples.

Even as the Father has loved me, I have also loved you. Remain in my love. If you keep my commandments, you will remain in my love, even as I have kept my Father's commandments and remain in his love.

I give to you a new commandment – that you love one another even as I have loved you. Just like I have loved you, you also should love one another. By this everyone will know that you are my disciples, if you have love for one another.

No one has greater love than this – that someone lay down his life for his friends.

I did not tell you these things from the beginning, because I was with you. But now I am going to him who sent me. Yet none of you asks me, *Where are you going?*

Thomas said to him, "Lord, we do not know where you are going. How can we know the way?"

Jesus said to him,

I came out from the Father and have come into the world. Again, I leave the world and go to the Father.

In my Father's house are many homes. If it were not so, I would have told you. I am going to prepare a place for you. If I go and prepare a place for you, I will come again and will receive you to myself, so that where I am, you may be there also. You know where I go, and you know the way.

Those who love me will keep my word. My Father will love them, and we will come to them and make our home with them. Whoever does not love me does not keep my words.

You are my friends if you do whatever I command you. No longer do I call you servants, for the servant does not know what the lord does. But I have called you friends, for I have made known to you everything that I heard from my Father.

If you love me, keep my commandments. I will pray to the Father, and he will give you another Redeemer, to be with you forever.

This is the Spirit of truth, whom the world cannot receive, for it neither sees him nor knows him. You know him, for he lives with you and will be in you.

I have yet many things to tell you, but you cannot bear them now. However, when the Spirit of truth comes, he will guide you into all truth, for he will not speak from himself but will speak whatever he hears. He will declare to you things that are coming.

I have spoken these things to you so that my joy may remain in you and that your joy may be made full. I command these things to you so that you may love one another.

Philip said to him, "Lord, show us the Father, and that will be enough for us."

Jesus said to him,

Have I been with you such a long time, and you do not know me, Philip? He who has seen me has seen the Father. How do you say, *Show us the Father?* Do you not believe that I am in the Father and the Father in me?

The words that I tell you, I speak not from myself, but the Father who lives in me does his works. Believe me that I am in the Father, and the Father in me, or else believe me for the sake of the very works.

Truly I tell you, the one who believes in me will also do the works that I do and will do greater works than these, because I am going to my Father.

I will do whatever you ask in my name, so that the Father may be glorified in the Son. If you will ask anything in my name, I will do it. He will glorify me, for he will take from what is mine and declare it to you. All things that the Father has are mine.

One who has my commandments and keeps them is one who loves me. One who loves me will be loved by my Father. I will love that one also and will reveal myself to him.

Judas, son of James, said to Jesus, "Lord, what has happened that you are about to reveal yourself to us and not to the world?"

Jesus answered him,

I will no longer speak much with you, for the prince of the world comes. He has nothing in me, but I do as the Father commanded me so that the world may know that I love the Father.

I have said these things to you while still living with you. But the Redeemer – the Holy Spirit that the Father will send in my name – will teach you all things and will remind you of all that I said to you.

When the Redeemer comes – the Spirit of truth that I will send to you from the Father – he will testify about me. You will also testify, because you have been with me from the beginning.

But because I have told you these things, sorrow has filled your heart. Nevertheless, I tell you the truth. It is to your advantage that I go away for, if I do not go away, the Redeemer will not come to you. But, if I go, I will send him to you.

When he comes, he will convict the world about sin, because they do not believe in me, and about righteousness, because I am going to my Father, and about judgment, because the prince of this world has been judged.

The word that you hear is not mine but is from the Father who sent me. Now arise, let us go from here.

Jesus speaks at Gethsemane

After Jesus had spoken these words, they sang a hymn. Then Jesus went out over the brook Kidron to a place named Gethsemane, on the Mount of Olives, where there was a garden, and his disciples followed him.

When they were at the place, Jesus said to them, "All of you will be made to stumble because of me tonight, for it is written, 'I will strike the shepherd, and the sheep of the flock will be scattered.' But after I am raised up, I will go before you into Galilee."

Simon said to him, "Lord, where are you going?"

Jesus answered, "Where I am going, you cannot follow now, but you will follow afterwards."

Simon said to him, "Lord, why can I not follow you now? Even if all will be made to stumble because of you, yet I will not. I am ready to go with you to prison and to death."

Jesus said to him, "Simon, Simon, behold. Satan asked to have you, that he might sift you as wheat, but I prayed for you that your faith would not fail. You, when once you have turned again, establish your brothers."

Simon said, "Lord, I will lay down my life for you."

Jesus answered, "Will you lay down your life for me? Truly I tell you, this night, before the rooster crows, you will deny three times that you know me."

Simon spoke all the more, "Even if I must die with you, I will not deny you." All of the disciples said the same thing.

He said to them, "When I sent you out without purse and wallet and shoes, did you lack anything?"

They said, "Nothing."

Then he said to them,

But now, whoever has a purse, take it, and likewise a wallet. Whoever has no sword, let him sell his cloak and buy one. I tell you, that which is written must still be fulfilled in me, *He was counted with the lawless.* That which concerns me has an end.

You did not choose me, but I chose you and appointed you to go and bear fruit – fruit that should remain – so that the Father may give to you whatever you will ask of him in my name.

If the world hates you, know that it hated me before it hated you. If you were of the world, the world would love its own. But, since I chose you out of the world, you are not of the world, and therefore the world hates you.

Remember the word that I said to you, *A servant is not greater than the lord.* If they persecuted me, they will also persecute you. If they kept my word, they will keep yours also. But all these things they will do to you for my name's sake, because they do not know him who sent me. If I had not come and spoken to them, they would not have sin, but now they have no excuse for their sin.

Whoever hates me hates my Father also. If I had not done among them the works that no one else did, they would not have sin. But now they have seen and hated both me and my Father. But this happened to fulfill the word that was written in their law, *They hated me without a cause.* I have said these things to you so that you would not be caused to stumble.

They will put you out of the synagogues. Yes, the time comes when those who kill you will think that they offer service to God. They will do these things because they have not known the Father nor me. But I have told you these things, so that when the time comes, you may remember that I told you about them.

In a little while, you will not see me. Again in a little while, you will see me. I have told you these things, so that in me you may have peace. In the world you have oppression but take heart, I have overcome the world. I do not give to you as the world gives. I give to you my peace. Peace I leave with you.

Some of his disciples said to one another, "What is this that he says to us, 'In a little while, you will not see me, and again in a little while, you will see me'? What is this that he says, 'Because I go to the Father'? We do not know what he is saying."

Jesus perceived that they wanted to ask him, and he said to them,

Do you inquire among yourselves about what I said, *In a little while, you will not see me, and again in a little while, you will see me?*

I will not leave you orphans – I will come to you. Yet in a little while the world will see me no more, but you will see me. Because I live, you will live also. On that day, you will know that I am in my Father and you in me and I in you.

Truly I tell you, you will weep and lament, but the world will rejoice. You will be sorrowful, but your sorrow will be turned into joy.

When a woman gives birth, she has sorrow, because her time has come. But when she has delivered the child, she does not remember the anguish anymore because of the joy that a human being is born into the world.

So you now have sorrow, but I will see you again and your hearts will rejoice and no one will take your joy away from you. On that day you will ask me no questions.

Truly I tell you, whatever you may ask of the Father in my name, he will give it to you. Until now, you have asked nothing in my name. Ask and you will receive, so that your joy may be made full.

I have spoken these things to you in figures of speech. But the time is coming when I will no longer speak to you in figures of speech but will tell you plainly about the Father. On that day you will ask in my name.

I do not say to you that I will pray to the Father for you, for the Father himself loves you, because you have loved me and have believed that I came forth from God.

His disciples said to him, "Behold, now you speak plainly and speak no figures of speech. Now we know that you know all things and do not need for anyone to question you. By this we believe that you came forth from God." Jesus answered them,

Do you now believe? Behold, the time is coming – yes, and has now come – that you will be scattered, everyone to his own place, and you will leave me alone. Yet I am not alone because the Father is with me.

I have yet many things to tell you, but you cannot bear them now. Just do not let your heart be troubled, neither let it be fearful. You heard how I told you, *I go away, and I come to you.* If you loved me, you would have rejoiced that I am going to my Father, for the Father is greater than I. Now I have told you before it happens so that, when it happens, you may believe.

Do not let your heart be troubled. Believe in God. Believe also in me.

Jesus prays before them

After Jesus said these things, he lifted up his eyes to heaven and said,

Righteous Father, the world does not know you, but I know you, and these know that you sent me. I made known your name to them and will make it known, so that the love with which you loved me may be in them, and I in them.

I revealed your name to the people whom you gave me out of the world. They were yours, and you gave them to me. They have kept your word. Now they know that all things you have given me are from you, for the words that you gave me I have given to them. They received them and know for sure that I came forth from you – they have believed that you sent me.

I have given them your word. The world hated them, because they are not of the world, even as I am not of the world. I pray that you would not take them from the world, but that you would keep them from the evil one.

I am no longer in the world, but these are in the world and I am coming to you. Holy Father, keep them through your name that you have given me, so that they may be one, even as we are.

While I was with them in the world, I kept them in your name. I have kept those whom you have given me. None of them is lost, except the son of destruction, so that the scripture might be fulfilled. But now I come to you, and I say these things in the world, so that they may have my joy made full in themselves.

All things that are mine are yours and yours are mine, and I am glorified in them. The glory that you have given me I have given to them, so that they may be one, even as we are one – I in them and you in me – that they may be perfected into one, so that the world may know that you sent me and loved them even as you loved me.

They are not of the world even as I am not of the world. Sanctify them in your truth – your word is truth. As you sent me into the world, even so I have sent them into the world. For their sakes I sanctify myself, so that they themselves also may be sanctified in truth.

I pray for them. I do not pray for the world but for those whom you have given me, for they are yours. Not for these only do I pray, but also for those who believe in me through their word, that they may all be one.

As you, Father, are in me and I in you, may they also be one in us, so that the world may believe that you sent me.

I glorified you on the earth. I have accomplished the work that you have given me to do. Now, Father, glorify me in your own self with the glory that I had with you before the world existed. Father, I desire that those you have given me also be with me where I am, so that they may see my glory from you, for you loved me before the foundation of the world.

Father, the time has come. Glorify your Son so that your Son may also glorify you. Even as you gave him authority over all flesh, he will give eternal life to all whom you have given him. This is eternal life, that they should know you – the only true God – and him whom you sent, Jesus the Messiah.

The hour has come

After this, he said to his disciples, "Sit here while I pray, and pray that you do not enter into temptation." He took with him Simon and James and John, the two sons of Zebedee. He began to be severely troubled and distressed. He said to them, "My soul is exceedingly sorrowful, even to death. Stay here, and watch with me."

He went forward a little, about a stone's throw from them, and fell on the ground and prayed that the hour might pass away from him. "My Father, if you are willing, remove this cup from me. Nevertheless, not my will, but yours, be done."

Then Jesus came back to the disciples and found them sleeping, and he said to Simon, "Could you not watch with me for one hour? Watch and pray, so that you do not enter into temptation. The spirit indeed is willing, but the flesh is weak."

He went away a second time and prayed, saying, "My Father, if this cup cannot pass away from me unless I drink it, your will be done."

He came again and found them sleeping, for their eyes were heavy, and they did not know what to say to him. He left them again, went away, and prayed a third time.

Being in agony, he prayed more earnestly. His sweat became like great drops of blood falling down on the ground. Then, an angel from heaven appeared to him, strengthening him.

When he rose up from his prayer, he came to the disciples, and said to them, "Sleep on now, and take your rest. It is enough. The hour has come – behold, the Son of Man is betrayed into the hands of sinners. Arise, let us be going. Behold, he who betrays me is at hand."

Jesus is betrayed

Judas, who betrayed him, knew the place where they were, for Jesus often met there with his disciples, and Judas brought a detachment of soldiers and a crowd from the chief priests, the scribes, the Pharisees, and elders of the people.

While Jesus was still speaking, they came there with lanterns, torches, swords, and clubs, and Judas was leading them.

Now the betrayer had given them a sign, saying, "Whoever I kiss, he is the one. Seize him and lead him away safely."

Immediately, Judas came near to Jesus, but Jesus said to him, "Judas, do you betray the Son of Man with a kiss? Friend, why are you here?"

Judas came to him and said, "Rabbi," and kissed him. Then they came and laid their hands on Jesus and took him.

Part 14

TRIAL AND CONVICTION

TRIAL AND CONVICTION

An account of events related to
the trial and conviction of Jesus the Messiah

Part 14

Jesus is arrested

AFTER THEY ARRESTED HIM, Jesus asked them, "Whom are you looking for?"

They answered, "Jesus of Nazareth."

Jesus said to them, "I am he. If therefore you seek me, let these go their way."

Then Simon stretched out his hand and drew his sword and struck the servant of the high priest, cutting off his right ear. The servant's name was Malchus, and Jesus immediately touched his ear and healed him and said,

> Put your sword back into its sheath, for all those who take the sword will die by the sword.
>
> Do you think that I could not ask my Father, and he would even now send me more than twelve legions of angels? But the cup that the Father has given me, shall I not surely drink it? How then would the scriptures be fulfilled that it must be so?

Then Jesus said to the crowd of chief priests, captains of the temple, and elders who had come against him,

> Have you come out as against a robber with swords and clubs to seize me? I sat daily with you in the temple teaching, and you did not stretch out your hands against me. But all this has happened so that the scriptures of the prophets might be fulfilled.
>
> This is your hour and the power of darkness.

Then all the disciples left him and fled.

Jesus is taken before Annas

The detachment, the commanding officer, and the officers of the Jews seized Jesus and bound him.

First they led him to Annas. He was father-in-law to Caiaphas, who was high priest that year and the one who advised the Jews that it was expedient that one man should perish for the people.

※ःःఎ※

A certain young man followed them, having a linen cloth thrown around himself over his naked body.

They grabbed him, but he left the linen cloth and fled from them naked.

※ःःఎ※

Annas, also a high priest, asked Jesus about his disciples and about his teaching.

Jesus answered, "I spoke openly to the world. I always taught in synagogues and in the temple, where the Jews meet. I said nothing in secret. Why do you ask me? Ask those who heard what I said to them. Behold, they know the things that I said."

When he had said this, one of the officers standing by slapped Jesus with his hand, saying, "Do you answer the high priest like that?"

Jesus answered, "If I have spoken evil, testify of the evil – but, if well, why do you beat me?"

Annas sent him bound to Caiaphas, the high priest.

Jesus is sent to Caiaphas

They seized him and led him away to the house of Caiaphas.

As soon as it was day, the assembly of the elders of the people, both chief priests and scribes, gathered together, and they led him into their council.

Now the chief priests, the elders, and the whole council sought testimony against Jesus, so that they might put him to death, and they found none. Many false witnesses came forward, and their testimony did not agree.

Some stood up, saying, "We heard him say, 'I will destroy this temple that is made with hands, and in three days I will build another made without hands.'" Two others came forward and said, "This man said, 'I am able to destroy the temple of God and to build it in three days.'" Even on this, their testimony did not agree.

The high priest stood up in their midst and asked Jesus, "What is it that these testify against you? Have you no answer?"

But Jesus held his peace and answered nothing.

Then the high priest said to him, "I adjure you by the living God – are you the Messiah, the Son of the Blessed God? If you are the Messiah, tell us."

Jesus said to them, "If I tell you, you will not believe and, if I ask, you will in no way answer. From now on, you will see the Son of Man seated at the right hand of the power of God and coming with the clouds of the sky."

They all asked, "Are you then the Son of God?"

He said to them, "You say it, because I am."

Then the high priest tore his clothing, saying, "He has spoken blasphemy. Why do we need any more witnesses? We ourselves have heard from his own mouth. What do you think?"

They all condemned him as they answered, "He is worthy of death."

✳

The men who held Jesus spat in his face and mocked him. Having blindfolded him, they beat him with their fists, and some slapped him, saying, "Prophesy to us, you Messiah. Who is the one who struck you?"

They spoke many other things against him and insulted him. The officers struck him with the palms of their hands.

Simon denies Jesus

When they led Jesus away to the high priest, Simon followed from a distance to the courtyard of the high priest.

The officers had kindled a fire of coals in the middle of the courtyard, for it was cold, and they were warming themselves. Entering in to see the end, Simon stood with them, warming himself in the light of the fire. When they sat down together, Simon sat among them.

They asked him, "You are not also one of his disciples, are you?"

He denied it, saying, "I am not."

As Simon was in the courtyard, one of the maids of the high priest came. She was a relative of the one whose ear Simon had cut off. Seeing him as he sat in the light warming himself, the servant girl looked at him intently, and said, "This man also was with Jesus, the Nazarene."

But Simon denied it before them all, saying, "Woman, I do not know what you are talking about. I do not know him." He went out on the porch.

❦

After a little while, one of those who stood by came and said to Simon, "Surely you are also one of them, for your speech makes you known – you are a Galilean."

Then Simon began to curse and to swear, and again he denied it with an oath, "I am not. I do not know this man of whom you speak."

❦

Immediately, while he was still speaking, a rooster crowed.

Then Simon remembered the word of the Lord, how Jesus said to him, "Before the rooster crows, you will deny me three times." When he thought about that, he wept bitterly.

Judas hangs himself

When Judas, the betrayer, saw that Jesus was condemned, he felt remorse and brought back the thirty pieces of silver to the chief priests and elders.

He said, "I have sinned – I betrayed innocent blood."

But they said, "What is that to us? You see to it."

He threw down the pieces of silver in the sanctuary and departed. He went away and hanged himself.

The chief priests took the pieces of silver and said, "It is not lawful to put them into the treasury, since it is the price of blood."

They took counsel and bought the potter's field with them as a place to bury strangers.

Jesus is sent to Pilate

When morning came, the chief priests, with the elders and scribes and the whole council, held a consultation in order to put Jesus to death. The whole company of them rose up, and they bound him and led him away to the governor's Praetorium and delivered him to Pontius Pilate.

They themselves did not enter into the Praetorium, so that they might not be defiled and kept from eating the Passover. Pilate therefore went out to them and said, "What accusation do you bring against this man?"

They answered him, "If this man were not an evildoer, we would not have delivered him up to you. We found this man perverting the nation, forbidding paying taxes to Caesar, and saying that he himself is the Messiah, a king."

Pilate said to them, "Take him yourselves and judge him according to your law."

The Jews replied, "It is not lawful for us to put anyone to death."

✺✺✺

Pilate entered the Praetorium and called Jesus and, as Jesus stood before the governor, Pilate asked him, "Are you the King of the Jews?"

Jesus answered, "Do you say this by yourself, or did others tell you about me?"

Pilate replied, "I am not a Jew, am I? Your own nation and the chief priests delivered you to me. What have you done?"

Jesus answered, "My kingdom is not of this world. If my kingdom were of this world, then my servants would fight, so that I would not be delivered to the Jews. But my kingdom is not from here."

So Pilate said to him, "Are you a king then?"

Jesus answered, "You say so. But for this reason I have been born, and for this reason I have come into the world – to testify to the truth. Everyone who is of the truth listens to my voice."

Pilate said to him, "Do you not hear how many things they testify against you? Have you no answer? What is the truth?"

But Jesus made no further answer, not even one word, and the governor marveled greatly.

Pilate went out again to the Jews and said to them, "I find no basis for a charge against this man. I will therefore chastise him and release him."

So Pilate took Jesus and flogged him. Then Pilate went out again and said to them, "Behold, I bring him out to you, so that you may know that I find no basis for a charge against him."

When Jesus came out, Pilate said to them, "Behold, the man."

When the chief priests and the officers saw him, they shouted, "Crucify. Crucify."

Pilate said to them, "Take him yourselves and crucify him, for I find no basis for a charge against him."

The Jews answered him, "We have a law, and by our law he ought to die because he made himself the Son of God."

When Pilate heard this, he was more afraid. He asked Jesus, "Where are you from?" But Jesus gave him no answer.

Pilate therefore said to him, "Are you not speaking to me? Do you not know that I have power to release you and power to crucify you?"

Jesus answered, "You would have no power at all against me unless it were given to you from above. Therefore the one who delivered me to you has greater sin."

The Jews insisted, saying, "He stirs up the people, teaching throughout all Judea, beginning from Galilee even to this place."

When Pilate heard Galilee mentioned, he asked if the man was a Galilean. And when he found out that Jesus was in Herod's jurisdiction, he sent him to Herod, who was also in Jerusalem during those days.

Herod returns Jesus to Pilate

When Herod saw Jesus, he was exceedingly glad, for he had wanted to see him for a long time, because he had heard many things about him. He hoped to see some miracle done by him.

Herod questioned him with many words, but Jesus gave no answers. The chief priests and the scribes stood, vehemently accusing him. Herod with his soldiers humiliated him and mocked him. Dressing him in luxurious clothing, they sent him back to Pilate.

Herod and Pilate became friends with each other that very day. Before this, they were enemies of each other.

⁂

Pilate called together the chief priests and the rulers and the people and said to them, "You brought this man to me as one that perverts the people. I have examined him before you and found no basis for a charge against this man concerning those things of which you accuse him. Neither has Herod, for he sent him to us. See, nothing worthy of death has been done by him. I will therefore chastise him again and release him."

But the Jews cried out, "If you release this man, you are not Caesar's friend. Everyone who makes himself a king speaks against Caesar."

Crucifixion is decided

Now at the feast the governor was accustomed to release to the crowd one prisoner, anyone for whom they asked. The crowd, crying aloud, began to ask Pilate to do as he always did for them.

At that time, they had a notable prisoner, called Barabbas, who was thrown into prison with those who committed murder during a revolt in the city.

When they were gathered together, Pilate said to them, "You have a custom that I release someone to you at the Passover." Perceiving that it was because of envy that they had delivered Jesus up, he said, "Do you want me to release to you the King of the Jews? Whom do you want me to release to you – Barabbas, or Jesus, who is called the Messiah – which of the two?"

While he was sitting on the judgment seat, Pilate's wife sent a message to him, saying, "Have nothing to do with that righteous man, for I have suffered many things this day in a dream because of him."

But the chief priests and the elders stirred up the crowd to ask for Barabbas and to have Jesus destroyed, and they shouted out together, "Not this man, but Barabbas. Away with this man. Release to us Barabbas."

Pilate again asked them, "What then should I do to Jesus, who is called the Messiah – him whom you call the King of the Jews?" They cried out, "Crucify him. Let him be crucified."

Pilate asked them, "Why? What evil has he done? I have found no capital crime in him."

Then Pilate, wanting to release Jesus, spoke to them again, but they shouted exceedingly, "Crucify. Crucify him. Let him be crucified. Crucify him."

They were urgent with loud voices, asking that he might be crucified. Their voices and the voices of the chief priests prevailed.

Pilate saw that nothing was being gained, but rather that a disturbance was starting. Wishing to please the crowd, he decreed that what they asked for should be done.

He released Barabbas – the man for whom they asked who had been thrown into prison for insurrection and murder, and he brought Jesus out and sat him down on the judgment seat at a place called Gabbatha.

Now it was the Preparation Day of the Passover at about the sixth hour. He said to the Jews, "Behold, your King."

They cried out, "Away with him. Away with him. Crucify him." Pilate asked them, "Shall I crucify your King?" The chief priests answered, "We have no king but Caesar."

Then Pilate took water and washed his hands before the crowd, saying, "I am innocent of the blood of this righteous person. You see to it."

All the people answered, "May his blood be on us and on our children."

After flogging Jesus, Pilate delivered him according to their will – to be crucified.

Part 15

CRUCIFIXION AND DEATH

CRUCIFIXION
AND DEATH

An account of events related to
the crucifixion and death of Jesus the Messiah

Part 15

The soldiers crucify Jesus

THE GOVERNOR'S SOLDIERS LED Jesus into the courtyard of the Praetorium, and they called together the whole cohort.

They stripped Jesus and clothed him with a scarlet robe and, weaving a crown of thorns, they put it on his head. Then the soldiers put a reed in his right hand, and they knelt down before him and mocked him – they saluted him, saying, "Hail, King of the Jews." At last, they spat on him, slapped him, and took the reed and struck him with it on the head.

After they had mocked him, they took the robe off of him and put his own garments on him. They led him away to crucify him. The soldiers also led away two others, who were criminals, to be put to death.

❦

As they led Jesus away, they found a man of Cyrene, Simon by name, the father of Alexander and Rufus, coming from the country, and they laid the cross on him to carry it after Jesus.

A great multitude of people followed him, including women who also mourned and lamented him. But Jesus turned to them and said,

> **Daughters of Jerusalem, do not weep for me, but weep for yourselves and for your children. For, behold, the days are coming in which they will tell the mountains, *Fall on us,* and tell the hills, *Cover us.* They will say, *Blessed are the barren, the wombs that never bore, and the breasts that never nursed.* If they do these things when the tree is green, what will be done when it is dry?**

Then, bearing his cross, Jesus went out, to the place called Golgotha. The soldiers offered him sour wine mixed with myrrh and gall, but he did not drink it.

There they crucified him.

※⁂※

Then the soldiers took his garments and divided the clothing among themselves, casting lots on them to determine what each should take.

Jesus said, "Father, forgive them, for they know not what they do."

The soldiers sat there and watched him.

Words are spoken at the cross

It was the third hour when they crucified Jesus, and with him they crucified the two criminals – one on either side – with Jesus in the middle.

One of the criminals hanging there insulted him, saying, "If you are the Messiah, save yourself and us."

But the other answered and, rebuking him, said, "Do you not even fear God, seeing you are under the same condemnation? And we indeed are treated justly, for we receive the due reward for our deeds, but this man has done nothing wrong."

Then he said to Jesus, "Lord, remember me when you come into your kingdom."

Jesus said to him, "Truly I tell you, today you will be with me in Paradise."

Pilate wrote the accusation against him, and they put it up on the cross over his head. It said, "Jesus of Nazareth, The King of the Jews," written in Hebrew, Latin, and Greek.

The place where Jesus was crucified was near the city, and many of the Jews read this inscription. Then the chief priests of the Jews said to Pilate, "Do not write, 'The King of the Jews,' but, 'He said, *I am King of the Jews.*'"

Pilate answered, "What I have written, I have written."

Those who passed by blasphemed Jesus, wagging their heads, and saying, "You who destroy the temple and build it in three days, save yourself. If you are the Son of God, come down from the cross."

The soldiers also mocked him, coming to him and offering him vinegar and saying, "If you are the King of the Jews, save yourself."

Likewise the chief priests, with the scribes, mocked him, saying, "He saved others, but let him save himself if this is the Messiah of God, his chosen one. If he is the King of Israel, let him come down from the cross now, and we will believe in him. He trusts in God — he said, 'I am the Son of God.' Let God deliver him now, if he wants him."

In the meantime, standing by the cross of Jesus were his mother, and his mother's sister, Mary the wife of Clopas, and Mary Magdalene.

When Jesus saw his mother, and the disciple whom he loved standing there, he said to his mother, "Woman, behold your son." Then he said to the disciple, "Behold, your mother." From that hour, the disciple took her to his own home.

Jesus breathes his last

It was now about the sixth hour, and darkness came over the whole land until the ninth hour. At the ninth hour, Jesus cried with a loud voice, "Eli, Eli, lama sabachthani?" – that is, "My God, my God, why have you forsaken me?"

Some of those who stood by, when they heard it, said, "Behold, he is calling Elijah. Let us see whether Elijah comes to take him down."

꧁꧂

After this, Jesus, knowing that all things were now finished, said, "I am thirsty."

It happened that a vessel full of vinegar was set there. Someone ran, filled a sponge full, then put the sponge on a reed, and held it to his mouth. When Jesus therefore had received the vinegar, he said, "It is finished."

He cried out with a loud voice, saying, "Father, into your hands I commit my spirit." Then he bowed his head, breathed his last, and gave up his spirit.

꧁꧂

At that time, behold, the veil of the temple was torn in two, from the top to the bottom. The earth quaked, and the rocks were split. The tombs were opened, and many bodies of the saints who had fallen asleep were raised.

When the centurion, who stood by opposite Jesus, saw what was done, he said, "Truly this man was the Son of God."

Those with him who were watching Jesus saw the earthquake and the way he cried out and breathed his last, and they feared exceedingly, saying, "Truly this was the Son of God."

Crucifixion is complete

When all the crowds that came together to witness this saw the things that were done, they returned home beating their breasts.

But all acquaintances of Jesus, including many women who came with him to Jerusalem, stood at a distance, watching these things.

The women who served him when he was in Galilee and who followed with him from there were among them and included Mary Magdalene, Mary – the mother of James and Joses – and Joanna and Salome – the mother of the sons of Zebedee.

❧

Because it was the Preparation Day – that is, the day before the sabbath – the Jews wanted it so that the bodies would not remain on the cross on the sabbath, especially that sabbath. Therefore, they asked of Pilate that the legs of the crucified might be broken and that they might be taken away.

So the soldiers came and broke the legs of the first and of the other who was crucified with Jesus.

But when they came to Jesus and saw that he was already dead, they did not break his legs. However, one of the soldiers pierced his side with a spear, and immediately blood and water came out.

Joseph entombs the body

Behold, there was a rich man named Joseph from Arimathaea, a city of the Jews, who, though a prominent member of the council, had not consented to their counsel and deed. He was a good and righteous man, waiting for the kingdom of God. He was also a disciple of Jesus, but secretly, for fear of the Jews.

When evening had come, Joseph of Arimathaea boldly went in to Pilate and asked if he might take away the body of Jesus.

Pilate marveled if Jesus were already dead and, summoning the centurion, he asked him whether Jesus had been dead long. When he found out what had happened from the centurion, he commanded that the body be granted to Joseph.

※豢溪豢

So Joseph came and took away the body.

Nicodemus, who at first came to Jesus by night, also came bringing a mixture of myrrh and aloes, about a hundred pounds.

They bound the body of Jesus with the spices in linen cloths, as is customary of the Jews.

Now there was a garden in the place where Jesus was crucified, with a new tomb, cut out in the rock, in which no one had ever yet been laid. They took the body and laid it there.

Joseph then rolled a great stone against the door of the tomb and departed.

Soldiers seal the tomb

The women who had come with Jesus out of Galilee were there. They saw where his body was laid and sat opposite the tomb. They prepared spices and ointments.

As the sabbath dawned, they rested according to the commandment.

❦

On the sabbath, the chief priests and the Pharisees were gathered together with Pilate and said, "Sir, we remember what that deceiver said while he was still alive – 'After three days I will rise again.' Command therefore that the tomb be made secure until the third day, lest perhaps his disciples come at night and steal him away and tell the people, 'He is risen from the dead.' This last deception would be worse than the first."

Pilate said to them, "You have a guard. Go, make it as secure as you can." So they went with the guard and made the tomb secure, sealing the stone.

Part 16

RESURRECTION

RESURRECTION

An account of events related to
the rising from the dead of Jesus the Messiah

Part 16

The tomb of Jesus is open

WHEN THE SABBATH WAS past, Mary Magdalene and the other Mary – the mother of James – bought spices, so that they might come and anoint Jesus.

On the first day of the week, at early dawn, while it was still dark, they went with the other women to the tomb where Jesus lay, bringing the spices that they had prepared.

They said among themselves, "Who will roll away the stone from the door of the tomb for us?"

But, looking up, they saw that the stone, which was very big, was already rolled away from the tomb. When they entered in, they did not find the body of the Lord Jesus, and they were greatly perplexed.

※彩彩※

Mary Magdalene ran to Simon and the other disciple, whom Jesus loved, and said to them, "They have taken the Lord out of the tomb, and we do not know where they have laid him."

Simon and the other disciple went out and ran together toward the tomb, but the other disciple outran Simon and came to the tomb first. Stooping and looking in, he saw the linen cloths lying there, yet he did not enter in.

Then Simon came, following him, and entered into the tomb. He saw the linen cloths lying there and the cloth that had been on Jesus' head – not lying with the linen cloths but rolled up in a place by itself.

So then the other disciple, who came first to the tomb, also entered in and believed that the Lord had been taken, for as yet they did not remember the scripture that he must rise from the dead.

Jesus appears to Mary Magdalene

But Jesus had risen early on the first day of the week, and he appeared first to Mary Magdalene, from whom he had cast out seven demons. He showed himself in this way.

※※※

While the disciples went away again to their own homes, Mary Magdalene stood outside the tomb, with the other women, weeping.

As she wept, she stooped and looked into the tomb and saw an angel of the Lord in dazzling clothing, white as snow, and she was amazed. He was sitting on the right side where the body of Jesus had lain, and his appearance was like lightning.

He said to her, "Woman, why are you weeping?"

She said to him, "Because they have taken away my Lord, and I do not know where they have laid him."

※※※

The guards who saw this were fearful of him – they shook and became like dead men. But Mary Magdalene and the other women entered the tomb, though terrified, with their faces bowed down to the earth.

The angel said to the women,

Do not be afraid. I know that you seek Jesus, the Nazarene, who has been crucified, but why do you seek the living among the dead?

He is not here, for he has risen – behold the place where the Lord was lying. Remember what he told you when he was still in Galilee – that the Son of Man must be delivered up into the hands of sinners and be crucified and on the third day rise again.

Go quickly and tell his disciples, *He has risen from the dead, and he goes before you into Galilee. There you will see him.*

Behold my words.

Trembling and astonishment came upon the women, and they went out and fled quickly from the tomb. They said nothing to anyone, for they were afraid.

⁂

But Mary Magdalene, after hearing the angel, turned around and saw Jesus standing there, but she did not know that it was he. Supposing him to be the gardener, she said to him, "Sir, if you have carried him away, tell me where you have laid him, and I will take him away."

Jesus said to her, "Mary. Rejoice."

She turned and said to him, "Rhabbouni," and she came to him, took hold of his feet, and worshiped him.

Jesus said to her, "Do not touch me, for I have not yet ascended to my Father. But go to my brothers and tell them that I am ascending to my Father and your Father, to my God and your God. Go tell my brothers that they should go into Galilee, and there they will see me."

⁂

Mary Magdalene departed with fear and great joy and found those who had been with him, as they mourned and wept. She told the disciples that she had seen the Lord and that he had said these things to her.

When they heard that he was alive and had been seen by her, these words seemed to them to be nonsense, and they did not believe them.

The priests devise an explanation

After Mary Magdalene left the tomb, some of the guards went into the city and told the chief priests all the things that had happened.

The chief priests took counsel when they were assembled with the elders, and they gave a large amount of silver to the soldiers and instructed them to say, "His disciples came by night and stole him away while we slept."

The priests also said to the soldiers, "If this comes to the governor's ears, we will persuade him and make you free of worry." So the soldiers took the money and did as they were told. This story was spread abroad among the Jews and continues to this day.

Jesus appears on walk to Emmaus

Behold, on that very day, Jesus was revealed in another form to two others as they walked on their way into the country to a village named Emmaus, which was sixty stadia from Jerusalem. They were talking with each other about all of the things that had happened.

While they talked and questioned together, Jesus himself came near and walked with them, but their eyes were kept from recognizing him.

He said to them, "What are you talking about as you walk, and why are you sad?"

One of them, named Cleopas, answered him, "Are you the only stranger in Jerusalem who does not know the things which have happened there in these days?"

He said to them, "What things?"

They answered, "The things concerning Jesus, the Nazarene, who was a prophet mighty in deed and word before God and all the people, and how the chief priests and our rulers delivered him up to be condemned to death and crucified him. But we were hoping that it was he who would redeem Israel.

"Besides all this, it is now the third day since these things happened. Also, certain women of our company amazed us. They arrived early at the tomb and, when they did not find his body, they came saying that they had also seen the vision of an angel who said that Jesus was alive. Some of our company went to the tomb and found it just like the women had said. But they did not see him."

Jesus said to them,

How foolish you are and slow of heart to believe in all that the prophets have spoken. Did not the Messiah have to suffer these things to enter into his glory?

Then, beginning from Moses and all the prophets, he explained to them in all the scriptures the things concerning himself.

※ЖѠ※

They drew near to the village where they were going, and he acted like he would go further.

They urged him, saying, "Stay with us, for it is almost evening, and the day is almost over."

He went in to stay with them and it happened that, when he had sat down at the table with them, he took the bread and gave thanks. Breaking it, he gave bread to them. At this, their eyes were opened, and they recognized him. But then he vanished out of their sight.

They said one to another, "Were not our hearts burning within us while he spoke to us along the way and opened the scriptures to us?"

※ЖѠ※

That very hour in the evening on that day – the first day of the week – they rose up and returned to Jerusalem and found where the eleven and those with them were gathered together.

They said, "The Lord is risen indeed and has appeared to us." They related the things that happened along the way and how Jesus was recognized by them in the breaking of the bread. But they did not believe them.

Jesus appears where the disciples gather

The doors were locked where the disciples were assembled for fear of the Jews. Yet, as they discussed these things, Jesus himself came and stood in their midst, and he rebuked them for their unbelief and hardness of heart, because they did not believe those who saw him after he had risen.

Then he said to them, "Peace be with you."

⁕≈≪⊙≫⁕

But they were terrified and filled with fear, and supposed that they had seen a spirit.

He said to them,

Why are you troubled? Why do doubts arise in your hearts? See my hands and my feet – that it is truly I. Touch me and see, for a spirit does not have flesh and bones, as you see that I have.

When he said this, he showed them his hands and his feet, and the disciples were glad when they saw the Lord.

While joyous, they wondered and still did not believe. He said to them, "Do you have anything here to eat?" They gave him a piece of a broiled fish and some honeycomb. He took them, and ate in front of them.

Then Jesus said to them again, "Peace be with you. As the Father has sent me, even so I send you." When he had said this, he breathed on them and said to them, "Receive the Holy Spirit. Whoever's sins you forgive, they are forgiven them. Whoever's sins you retain, they will be retained."

⁕≈≪⊙≫⁕

Thomas, one of the twelve, called Didymus, was not with them when Jesus came. The other disciples therefore said to him, "We have seen the Lord."

But he said to them, "Unless I see in his hands the print of the nails and put my hand into his side, I will not believe."

⚜

After eight days, the disciples were again inside, and Thomas was with them. Though the doors were locked, Jesus came and stood in the midst and said, "Peace be with you."

Then he said to Thomas, "Reach your finger here and see my hands. Reach your hand here and put it into my side. Do not be unbelieving, but believing."

Thomas answered him, "My Lord and my God."

Jesus said to him, "You have believed because you have seen me, Thomas. Blessed are those who have not seen and have believed."

Jesus appears by the sea at Tiberias

After these things, Jesus revealed himself again to the disciples at the sea of Tiberias. He revealed himself this way.

Simon, Thomas called Didymus, Nathanael of Cana in Galilee, the sons of Zebedee, and two others of his disciples were together.

Simon said to them, "I am going fishing," and they told him, "We are also coming with you." They went out and entered into the boat. That night, they caught nothing.

When day had just come, Jesus stood on the beach, yet the disciples did not know that it was Jesus. He said to them, "Children, have you anything to eat?" They answered him, "No."

He said to them, "Cast the net on the right side of the boat, and you will find some." So they cast it, and now they were not able to draw it in for the multitude of fish.

The disciple whom Jesus loved said to Simon, "It is the Lord."

When Simon heard that it was the Lord, he wrapped his coat around him, for he was naked, and threw himself into the sea. But the other disciples came in the little boat, dragging the net full of fish, for they were not far from the land — only about two hundred cubits away.

So when they got out on the land, they saw a fire of coals there, with fish laid on it, and bread. Jesus said to them, "Bring some of the fish that you have just caught."

Simon went up and drew the net to land, full of great fish — one hundred fifty-three — and, even though there were so many, the net was not torn.

Jesus said to them, "Come and eat breakfast."

None of the disciples dared inquire of him, "Who are you?" knowing that it was the Lord. Then Jesus came and took the bread, gave it to them, and the fish likewise.

This is now the third time that Jesus was revealed to his disciples after he had risen from the dead.

❦

The disciples remembered that Jesus had said, "Destroy this temple, and in three days I will raise it up," speaking of the temple of his body.

They now believed the scripture and the word that Jesus had said.

✳✳✳

When they had eaten their breakfast, Jesus said to Simon, "Simon, son of Jonah, do you love me more than these?" Simon said to him, "Yes, Lord, you know that I have affection for you." And Jesus said to him, "Feed my lambs."

He said to him again a second time, "Simon, son of Jonah, do you love me?" Simon answered, "Yes, Lord, you know that I have affection for you." And Jesus said to him, "Tend my sheep."

Then he said to him the third time, "Simon, son of Jonah, do you have affection for me?" Simon was grieved because he asked him three times, and he said to him, "Lord, you know everything. You know that I have affection for you."

Jesus said to him, "Feed my sheep. Truly I tell you, when you were young, you dressed yourself and walked where you wanted. But when you are old, you will stretch out your hands and another will dress you and carry you where you do not want to go."

He said this, signifying by what kind of death he would glorify God. After he had said this, Jesus said to Simon, "Follow me."

✳✳✳

Then Simon, turning around, saw a disciple following. This was the disciple whom Jesus sincerely loved – the one who had also leaned on Jesus' breast at the supper and asked, "Lord, who is going to betray you?"

Seeing him, Simon said to Jesus, "Lord, what about this man?"

Jesus said to him, "If I desire that he stay until I come, what is that to you? You follow me."

This saying therefore went out among the people that this disciple would not die.

Jesus speaks in Galilee

The eleven disciples went into Galilee, to the mountain where Jesus had first sent them. When they saw him, they bowed down to him.

Having loved his own who were in the world, Jesus loved them to the end. He came near to them and said, "This is what I told you, while I was still with you – that all things written concerning me in the law of Moses, the prophets, and the psalms must be fulfilled."

Then he opened their minds, so that they might understand the scriptures. He said to them,

Thus it is written that it was necessary for the Messiah to suffer and to rise from the dead on the third day and that repentance and remission of sins should be proclaimed in his name to all the nations, beginning at Jerusalem.

You are witnesses of these things. Behold, I send forth the promise of my Father on you. But wait in the city of Jerusalem until you are clothed with power from on high. Then go, and make disciples of all nations, baptizing them in the name of the Father and of the Son and of the Holy Spirit.

These signs will accompany those who believe – they will speak with new languages, they will lay hands on the sick and they will recover, they will cast out demons in my name, they will take up serpents, and, if they drink any deadly thing, it will in no way hurt them.

The one who believes and is baptized will be saved, but the one who disbelieves will be condemned.

All authority has been given to me in heaven and on earth. Therefore, go into all the world and proclaim the good news to the whole creation, teaching them to observe all things that I commanded you.

Behold, I am with you always, even to the end of the age.

Jesus the Messiah is glorified

So then the Lord Jesus, after he had spoken to them, led them out, and he lifted up his hands and blessed them. While he did this, he withdrew from them and was carried up into heaven. He sat down at the right hand of God.

❦

The disciples returned to Jerusalem with great joy, and they worshiped him. They were continually in the temple, praising and blessing God. Then they went out and proclaimed everywhere, while the Lord worked with them and confirmed the Word by the signs that followed.

Amen.

AFTERWORD

Come to the Light

GOD SO LOVED THE world that he gave his one and only Son, so that whoever believes in him should not perish but have eternal life.

God did not send his Son into the world to judge the world but in order that the world should be saved through him.

Those who believe in him are not judged, but those who do not believe have been judged already, because they have not believed in the name of the one and only Son of God.

This is the judgment – that the light has come into the world, and people loved the darkness rather than the light, for their works were evil. Those who do evil hate the light and do not come to the light, lest their works be exposed.

But those who act in truth come to the light, so that their works may be revealed as having been done in God.

GENEALOGY

Genealogy of Jesus the Messiah

An account of the genealogy of Jesus the Messiah
— the son of David, the son of Abraham, the son of Adam, the Son of God —

All the generations of fathers from Abraham to David are fourteen generations, from David to the exile to Babylon, fourteen generations, and from the exile to Babylon to the Messiah, fourteen generations.

1.	**Abraham** ⅂	Solomon[5] ⅂	Shealtiel ⅂
2.	Isaac ⅂	Rehoboam ⅂	Zerubbabel ⅂
3.	Jacob ⅂	Abijah ⅂	Abiud ⅂
4.	Judah[1] ⅂	Asa ⅂	Eliakim ⅂
5.	Perez[2] ⅂	Jehoshaphat ⅂	Azor ⅂
6.	Hezron ⅂	Joram ⅂	Sadoc ⅂
7.	Ram ⅂	Uzziah ⅂	Achim ⅂
8.	Amminadab ⅂	Jotham ⅂	Eliud ⅂
9.	Nahshon ⅂	Ahaz ⅂	Eleazar ⅂
10.	Salmon ⅂	Hezekiah ⅂	Matthan ⅂
11.	Boaz[3] ⅂	Manasseh ⅂	Jacob ⅂
12.	Obed[4] ⅂	Amon ⅂	Joseph, the father,
13.	Jesse ⅂	Josiah ⅂	as was supposed,
14.	**King David** ⅃	Jechoniah[1,6] ⅃	of **Jesus**
			who is called
			The Messiah

⅂⅃ - the father of

[1]and his brothers   [2]and Zerah, by Tamar   [3]by Rahab
[4]by Ruth   [5]by her who had been the wife of Uriah
[6]at the time of the exile to Babylon

The fathers of Mary are recorded to the beginning of man.

1.	**God** ⅂	Hezron ⅂	Cosam ⅂
2.	**Adam** ⅂	Arni ⅂	Addi ⅂
3.	Seth ⅂	Admin ⅂	Melchi ⅂
4.	Enos ⅂	Amminadab ⅂	Neri ⅂
5.	Cainan ⅂	Nahshon ⅂	Shealtiel ⅂
6.	Mahalaleel ⅂	Salmon ⅂	Zerubbabel ⅂
7.	Jared ⅂	Boaz ⅂	Rhesa ⅂
8.	Enoch ⅂	Obed ⅂	Joanan ⅂
9.	Methuselah ⅂	Jesse ⅂	Judah ⅂
10.	Lamech ⅂	David ⅂	Joseph ⅂
11.	Noah ⅂	Nathan ⅂	Semein ⅂
12.	Shem ⅂	Mattatha ⅂	Mattathias ⅂
13.	Arphaxad ⅂	Menan ⅂	Maath ⅂
14.	Cainan ⅂	Melea ⅂	Naggai ⅂
15.	Shelah ⅂	Eliakim ⅂	Esli ⅂
16.	Eber ⅂	Jonan ⅂	Nahum ⅂
17.	Peleg ⅂	Joseph ⅂	Amos ⅂
18.	Reu ⅂	Judah ⅂	Mattathias ⅂
19.	Serug ⅂	Simeon ⅂	Joseph ⅂
20.	Nahor ⅂	Levi ⅂	Jannai ⅂
21.	Terah ⅂	Matthat ⅂	Melchi ⅂
22.	Abraham ⅂	Jorim ⅂	Levi ⅂
23.	Isaac ⅂	Eliezer ⅂	Matthat ⅂
24.	Jacob ⅂	Jose ⅂	Heli, the father
25.	Judah ⅂	Er ⅂	of Mary,
26.	Perez ⅃	Elmodam ⅃	from whom **Jesus** was born, who is called **The Messiah**

⅂⅃ - the father of

There were disciples who testified about these things, and we know that their witness is true. But Jesus did many other things and gave many other signs in the presence of his disciples which are not written in this book. If they were fully recorded, the world itself could not hold all the books that would be written.

Design Attributions

The cover of the *Millennium Reader's Edition* of **The Common Gospel** was designed by Mark Mickel and Bill Chiaravalle of Brand Navigation, LLC.

The *Key to Knowledge* photograph that appears on the cover is copyrighted by Coston Stock / Alamy and is used with permission.

The character set used throughout the text is a version of the classic Bronte typeface distributed by SWFTE International, and the symbol used as a section separator is from the Fleurons ornamental fontset designed by Stephen Moye.

The interior design of **The Common Gospel**, including the map of the region, was completed by R. M. MEBANE, Editor. The book is printed on 60-pound opaque cream paper.

About the Editor

R. M. MEBANE is formally credentialed in letters by Swarthmore College (B.A.) and the University of Pennsylvania's Annenberg School of Communication (M.A.).

Over the course of his career, Mr. Mebane has shown a penchant for finding inherent structure in complex systems and constructs. In another public work, for example, he contained the grammatical rules of a modern Romance language in fewer than one-hundred pages of text. (*Más Fácil: A Concise Review of Spanish Grammar*, Prentice Hall, with E. Calderón-Young.)

Mr. Mebane currently works as a master wordsmith in the Chicago suburb of Geneva, Illinois, where he is also an active proponent of beekeeping and wood carving. His editorial work on *The Common Gospel* spanned a twelve-year period (1992-2004).

Communication

Direct all correspondence regarding *The Common Gospel* to:

Wordsmith Associates
1400 Sherwood Lane
Geneva, IL 60134
United States of America
RMEBANE@WORDSMITH.ASSOCIATES

For information on *The Common Gospel*, including how to obtain additional copies, visit: HTTPS://WORDSMITH.ASSOCIATES.

Printed in the USA
CPSIA information can be obtained
at www.ICGtesting.com
LVHW041630061024
793058LV00001B/29